THE CITY

Books by John V. Lindsay

JOURNEY INTO POLITICS

THE CITY

THE CITY

John V. Lindsay

W · W · NORTON & COMPANY · INC ·
NEW YORK

SBN 393 05387 3

FIRST EDITION

 Published simultaneously in Canada by George J. McLeod Limited, Toronto. *Library of Congress Catalog Card No. 68–54968.* Printed in the United States of America.

1 2 3 4 5 6 7 8 9 0

For Kathy, Margie, Anne, and Johnny,
whose father has missed too many dinners
and too many evenings, and who have returned
his preoccupation with patience and love

Contents

Acknowledgments

THERE IS no end to the list of persons who contributed, each in some way, to the writing of this book. Essentially, it is the product of very long weeks and hours spent in the urban struggle. And there are many, many persons who have shared that struggle with me. They begin with my wife, Mary, and my four children, who have been loving, supportive, and patient. And they end with a tolerant and understanding electorate, which has now returned me to the struggle.

Most especially, for the assistance I have had in the writing, rewriting, and writing again of this book, my thanks go to my assistant, Jeff Greenfield, to my press secretary, Thomas Morgan, and to a small staff of young mayoral assistants who inexhaustibly, each day and night, with skill and good humor, put business before pleasure.

There are, also, two very old friends, Evan Thomas and Eric Swenson, who have published this book, and who, too, have lived these long years with me.

Finally, my thanks go to Richard Aurelio, my campaign manager in the 1969 campaign for Mayor, who held the ship together in the most turbulent seas I have yet sailed.

J.V.L.

I

The Struggle for New York

NEW YORK *is not like any other place. As one writer has said, it is not four Philadelphias or fifty-five New Havens. It is New York. It is larger in population than all but two states. It has five boroughs—if you split the city up, you would have four of the five largest cities in the United States. It has a police force larger than the entire federal law-enforcement force—the police budget is greater than Detroit's entire city budget. It runs, and largely pays for, its own university—one of the five largest in the world. It has every ethnic group that has ever come to the United States, often living in unwanted proximity to each other. It is the melting pot that has yet to melt—a coalescence of dozens of different races, religions, and nationalities, each with traditions jealously guarded and each seeking a measure of autonomy and respect.*

New York City has more facets of joy and sorrow than any other city. It has the most robust economy in America—and a million people on welfare. It has some of the most beautiful urban neighborhoods in the country—and some of the worst slums imaginable. It has the greatest health facilities in the world—and some of its people die because they do not get treatment. It has more children in its schools than anywhere else—and too many of them do not learn.

New York has moments, especially in spring and fall, when you would not live in any other place in the world.

It has moments in summer and winter when you would leave it forever. It has some of the proudest people you can find, who will tell you that "when you leave New York, it's all Bridgeport" (apologies to Bridgeport). And it has people who will tell you that the city should sink into the Atlantic Ocean tomorrow for the sake of civilization.

It has subways—now—that carry passengers in air-conditioned comfort, and it has subways that turn a summer day into living hell. It has the best and largest police force anywhere in the world, and it has crime, far too much crime for the serenity of its citizens. It has a half a dozen specialized high schools that produce the best-educated youth possible, and it has schools where fourteen-year-old children shoot heroin.

It has, in other words, the promise and the danger of urban America: the promise of becoming a still greater city, the danger of falling victim to steady, certain decay. I've been Mayor of it for four years—and, as this book is published, I've just become Mayor of it again.

In some ways, the business of being Mayor of New York City is the most frustrating in the country. His burdens have been described as being second only to that of the President. But a President is recognized as a man with an awesome burden, and many of his most pressing problems are far away from the immediate concerns of the people. But a Mayor is the chief executive of the first line of government. It's his responsibility to see that there are enough police on the streets, modern and sufficient schools, comfortable transportation, heat in the winter, and adequate housing. The things a Mayor does or does not do touch the daily life of people; when his level of government does not work effectively, he feels directly the discontent of his constituency. He also feels it when another level of government does not work effectively.

A Mayor, moreover, is the chief executive of a stepchild form of government. The states are an integral part of our constitutional framework. The United States is, after all, a federal union of states—sovereign states, we are reminded at every political convention. But a city does not exist by constitutional guarantee. It is the creature of a state, subject to its mandate. It cannot raise its resources according to its lights, raise its debt ceiling, change its tax base, or change the way its government works without approval of the state. It is, in other words, a governmental unit without direct access to power obliged to take direct responsibility for the problems of people.

The ultimate problem is money—or, rather, the problem of not enough money. Whatever else a city can do, it cannot provide the services its people want if it does not have the money to pay for them. And our cities don't have the money. There is no other business I can think of where the proprietor knows absolutely *that he will face bankruptcy every year. Yet my own city's expenses—with no increase at all in programs—go up each year three times as much as revenues. That does not make for tranquillity. It does make for citizens who must wonder every year whether their local library will cut back its hours, whether their children will be forced to attend split sessions in the schools, whether their hospital can be modernized to meet inevitably higher demands.*

These kinds of needs mean that another mayoral bur-

jobs, funding recreation and educational experiments that have achieved astonishing success.

• Most of all, I've seen individual citizens come to realize that they can change the course of city government, and the quality of their own lives, by investing their own time and energy. I've seen this spirit take hold and flourish in an age when citizens are supposed to have stopped caring about their own communities.

I have, of course, seen and heard other things as well. I have heard angry citizens protesting outside City Hall against policies they did not like. I've heard shouts of fury and anger against races and religions. I've heard accusations that I have sold out, or betrayed the city, or failed to do anything. And I've heard people say that New York cannot be governed, that it is doomed to stay a city where you cannot travel through midtown in comfort, where you cannot walk the streets safely, where you cannot find a decent place to live at a price you can afford, where you cannot breathe or work or play or rest in confidence.

But I think the voices of pessimism are in the wrong city. I think I can see that if—if—New York and its sister cities get the resources they need, if—if—the federal government recognizes the city as an urgent priority for the nation, we can build the kind of city that will capture the best this town has within it. We can turn the enormous energy and intelligence of this city's people into the most powerful force for change we have ever seen. We can make this a city where each separate, unique neighborhood is vibrant with the energy of its own citizenry, at work in a common effort of turning their com-

munities into places of hope and satisfaction.

That is not a dream. That kind of city is a necessity. It is also a possibility. It is something that can be done—in spite of all the cynicism that a town like this can breed.

I believe it now more deeply than I did when I first became Mayor. I think New York can lead this country into an age of urban greatness, if we have the chance.

I

Election 1969

IT WAS DURING the summer of 1969, shortly before Labor Day, which traditionally kicks off the New York mayoral campaign. A *New York Times* reporter gave one of my aides his estimate of my re-election chances.

"If John Lindsay wins against Mario Procaccino," he said, "it will be like Montclair State Teachers College beating Notre Dame."

That reflects the general atmosphere in which my fall campaign began. I was seeking a second term without the support of the Republican or Democratic parties. State Senator John Marchi had beaten me in the Republican primary in June by 6,000 votes. My opponent on the Democratic line, Controller Mario Procaccino, was between ten and fifteen points ahead of me in polls taken after the primaries. And, beyond the polls, in a city where seven out of ten voters are registered Democrats, any Democratic candidate had to be assumed the favorite.

But more important, it was clear that a broad segment of the electorate felt a special ill will toward me. Indeed, it seemed I had managed to unite a wide variety of New Yorkers in a common cause: my retirement. The *Times*man could not be blamed for his prediction.

There was, then, a well-founded pessimism prevailing among my supporters—and in my own mind. The reasons for my low state are worth looking at, because they tell us something important about the nature of New York City.

The last six months of 1968 had been the worst of my public life. At one point, for about a week (on top of many weeks earlier), the schools were shut down in a bitter teachers' strike, the police were engaged in work slowdowns, the firemen and sanitationmen were threatening similar "job actions," and a flu epidemic was heading straight for the city. More fundamentally, the tensions between racial and religious groups in New York were breaking to the surface in an angry series of verbal and emotional confrontations. Two historic allies in progressive causes—the black and the Jewish communities—were looking at each other with suspicion and hostility. And, as this tension was brought to the surface during the school dispute, it was turning an already emotional labor dispute into a traumatic conflict.

I was both too close and, perhaps, too far away from the 1968 school strike for complete objectivity. What can be said is that the roots of the teachers' strike were buried in a clash between two forces with essentially legitimate goals: residents of the black and Puerto Rican neighborhoods, who were demanding a school system that could communicate with and educate their children; and the teachers and supervisors of the school system, who wanted protection for their personal safety and professional rights.

A dispute between an experimental, neighborhood-run public school district in a black neighborhood in Brooklyn and a group of union teachers in that district had precipitated the strike. Because of an initial mistake in establishing these districts solely in black and Puerto Rican neighborhoods—a mistake for which I bear my share of the responsibility—the dispute took on ugly racial and religious overtones. The local school governing board was almost all black and Puerto Rican. The majority of New York teachers are Jewish. A handful of black extremists resorted to anti-white and anti-Semitic epithets. A few teachers and their supporters resorted to more implicit, but still ugly, anti-black tactics. When the dispute erupted into a citywide strike, the overtones of a racial-religious clash were swept into the mainstream of city concern. Rumors were spread of white racism among teachers, of extreme black-power sentiments among black leadership, of my own intention to appoint a notorious black extremist to the Board of Education. And even after a settlement was reached, the hostilities stirred up took a long time to subside. What was too often forgotten on both sides was that the warring factions—teacher and parent alike—had right on their side. What was remembered was a lengthy, bitter shutdown of the city's schools and a direct clash between racial groups in the city.

A number of other events, less critical to the city but politically serious for me, darkened the period for me. At the end of 1968, in the midst of a Hong Kong flu epidemic, a fuel strike hit the city. The day *after* it was settled, I went off with my family for a short vacation. But full deliveries had not been resumed, and though the crisis was actually over, the implication was that I had left a shivering city in crisis for a vacation in the sun. And in February of 1969 the worst snowstorm in twenty years hit New York suddenly and without warning on a Sunday, and it hit with particular force in eastern Queens. Again, a whole raft of factors—including lack of warning, inadequate preparation, and, in one instance, explicit work-force sabotage—stranded thousands of people for days. The day after the storm I went out to the most affected neighborhoods, and the reception I got was virtually unanimous. There were a number of suggestions about what I might do with myself, and there was a good deal of fascinating speculation about my ancestry.

Combined with these specific incidents was a more basic, less well-defined backlog of complaints. Diverse as they were, they centered around a common theme that for personal or ideological reasons I had neglected the middle class of New York City in favor of the Manhattan affluent and the poor, especially the black poor. Among many New Yorkers early in 1969 you were likely to hear something like this about my administration:

"John Lindsay doesn't care about the typical, hardworking man who lives in Brooklyn, Queens, or the Bronx. All he cares about is his national image because he wants to run for President. He wants to keep the city cool, so he pays off the blacks with welfare and poverty money, and he ties the hands of police by letting his young assistants interfere with police who try to stop rioters and criminals.

"Meanwhile, the store owner, the housewife, the teachers are afraid in the streets, in the schools, in their shops.

"All Lindsay knows is Manhattan. He still thinks he's a Congressman from the Silk Stocking district. He doesn't know anything about the other boroughs. He can't even clean the streets or get us out of a snowstorm. All his fancy talk about reorganizing the government means is that his Wall Street friends can get high-paying city jobs while he goes on television and lets the city go to hell.

"He keeps the blacks happy by putting them on welfare and by walking through their neighborhoods. And he protects his wealthy friends by encouraging militants to attack the middle-class New Yorker."

There were of course a great many more specific complaints: the subways were crowded and often delayed, the streets were dirty, taxes were too high. Sometimes the link between my responsibility and the grievance became a bit attenuated, such as my failure to get the Long Island Railroad to run on time, my insidious plot to break every pay telephone within the city limits, and my permissive morality, which sent thousands of girls out on city streets without brassieres. And sometimes I felt a strong urge to protest vigorously and discuss the record. My protection of the wealthy, for example, had included the first tax on bank profits in city history, the raising of the stock-transfer tax and corporate taxes in general, and court fights against the utilities, Blue Cross, and the telephone company.

But that kind of protest had to be largely irrelevant. The fact was that for a complex series of reasons rooted in attitudes toward my personality, the very real difficulties, economic and otherwise, of most New Yorkers, and the physical conditions around the city, a great many New Yorkers—almost certainly a majority—wanted me out as Mayor. And it became apparent first of all that unless I could demonstrate some recognition of the real grievances at the root of this disaffections, I could not win re-election —and indeed I would not deserve to win. But I, together with those of my aides with political responsibility, knew something else: that it was neither responsible nor prudent to appeal to the fears of these New Yorkers. This was too simple and too dangerous. Victory would not be worth that price. As it turned out, I think, the right decision was, at least this time, the right political decision as well.

By early 1969 a political columnist who had declared me unbeatable a few months earlier was assuring his readers that under no circumstances would I run for re-election. The pressures, he said, were too great, the odds against re-election too strong, other pastures beckoned.

There was a good deal of irony for me in this fall from grace. Not six months earlier, in August 1968, the choice was mine whether to leave the Mayor's office for the Senate seat of the late Robert Kennedy. This came after the Republican convention in Miami, which I survived, and at a time when my political fortunes were high.

Turning it down wasn't easy, but accepting a federal appointment—even to a Senate seat—struck me as an abandonment of the city, and especially of the people I had talked into joining the fight for the city at a time of great stress. Further, any such move seemed to me then as a retreat from the real fight. Conversely, saying no signaled a sense of importance about the "mayoring" business.

Still, I was very conscious of how precarious my political strength had become (although I cannot claim to any clairvoyance about the disastrous fall). A phone conversation with my friend, former New Haven Mayor Richard Lee, particularly stands out in my mind as a reflection of that time.

"Take my advice, take the Senate seat," Dick said. "You can't possibly win in your job; none of us can. Get out while you can." This advice came from a man who had been Mayor of New Haven for fourteen years, and one of the nation's great mayors. But the New Haven race riots of 1967 had embittered him. He, along with seven other mayors of major American cities, declined to run for re-election in 1969.

By 1969 the temptation to quit at the end of my first term was very strong. Part of it was simply personal. The pressures of the office were equally great, if not greater, on my wife. We could not lead a natural home life. We have four children, of whom I had seen far too little for the last four years; the demands of the job are virtually unrelenting. But more importantly, perhaps, the fundamental problem of the city—the lack of resources to do the job that needs doing—was no nearer to resolution. Washington, particularly, seemed uninterested in the city. Given those circumstances, Dick Lee's example seemed about right. Mayor of New York was a job that promised a lot more torment and little possibility of making basic and vitally needed changes in the life of the city.

The arguments to run, however, were also compelling.

I had started a number of programs and projects that I wanted to see completed; although it's hard to realize, some of the first programs I launched as Mayor will not be finished until after the end of my second term. Moreover, I felt strongly that an advocate-mayor was essential if there was to be any hope of change in state and federal attitudes. I had argued for four years that people had to be willing to make this fight. To leave now would suggest a sense of total defeat which—even in the worst days of 1968—I did not feel.

Another argument, neglected by almost every political commentator, was that I wanted the chance to set right some of the things that had gone wrong. Despite the long walks in the streets, a much broader base of decision making was needed in all the neighborhoods of New York, and there were programs that hadn't worked and that needed to be changed. Finally, as Mayor I was a little wiser than in 1965. The White Knight had been tarnished a good deal, but at least he could tell the difference between windmills and real dragons.

Ultimately, I decided to run again (it is *not* true that the real reason for this decision was the lack of middle-income housing for a family of six). On February 4, in announcing my intention to seek re-election, I said two things that were to become important themes of the whole campaign: first, "I won't pretend my administration has been without error or mistakes"; second, "I would rather lose with what I believe in than win by betraying my principles and this city."

Shortly after I announced, one of my assistants—a Democrat—said, "You know, what I really hope is that you lose this damn primary and run on your own." I could have assured him then that it was my judgment and those of my closest advisers that he was going to get his wish.

Discontent among Republicans had been apparent from the early days of my administration, when I began to make a practice of choosing Democrats, Liberals, and independents as well as Republicans for city jobs and appointments. In addition, I had taken many stands—ranging from civil rights to poverty to Vietnam to civil liberties—which were in sharp disagreement with many GOP state legislators and councilmen, who in turn made no secret of their disagreements.

After the school strike and the other events of 1968, the prospect of a primary opponent became apparent. The Governor, it was clear, would not stand in his way, and the Lieutenant Governor, anxious to become a governor himself some day, would in fact encourage him.

The principal opponent turned out to be a man about whom most New Yorkers knew little—and that in many ways was one of his assets. He was John Marchi, a state senator from Staten Island, New York's fifth borough and totally unlike any other part of the city. Senator Marchi had a twelve-year record in the state Senate and had close relations with the upstate Republican leadership. As chairman of the New York City Affairs Committee, he had been instrumental in passing the school bill that had delayed a legislative decision on school decentralization. He had usually supported the upstate party leaders during fights between the city and state for more aid to the city. His record, however, was incidental. His real asset

—in addition to a low-keyed, amiable campaign style—was that he was not John Lindsay.

When he entered the primary, Marchi had the support of the key legislative and executive leadership of the state party and the explicit support of the Conservative Party, a growing force in the state whose support guaranteed him a place on the ballot in November. For a time, a third candidate in the mayoral primary race, State Assemblyman Vito Battista of Brooklyn, appeared to be taking votes from Marchi, but toward the end of the campaign he dropped out to run for controller on Marchi's ticket. That decision meant two things—first, it substantially lowered the decible volume of the mayoral race; second, it unified the opposition to me within the Republican Party. And it thus made Marchi an even more potent threat.

Candidly, it has to be said that Marchi seemed likely to appeal to New York City Republicans, insofar as anyone knew anything about them. There had not been a city Republican primary since 1941, when Fiorello LaGuardia was challenged by a conservative who charged that he had handcuffed the police and given the city over to Harlem. What we did know was that there were about 625,000 registered Republicans; that they were, on the average, over the age of fifty; that the largest ethnic group among them were Italian-Americans, who had been drawn into the party years before; and that most of them lived outside of Manhattan. Not precisely a liberal mayor's constituency!

Research told us that my own candidacy of necessity had to look beyond the primary. As one who had been elected promising a fusion government, I was seeking a ticket for my second term that would in fact reflect this policy. Thus, I asked Sanford Garelik, the Chief Inspector of the New York police force and a registered Democrat, to run as City Council president, and Fiorvante Perrotta, my Finance Administrator and a progressive Republican, to run for controller. It was a good ticket, but in a rough Republican primary the presence of a Democrat could not (I thought then) help.

The most significant encouragement I had during this period was the support of the Liberal Party and its chairman, Alex Rose. For twenty-five years the Liberal Party had been a third force in the city and state, supporting both Republicans and Democrats (usually the latter) for public office. The Liberal Party had supported me in 1965, but by the spring of 1969 some party members (many of whom, as labor union officials, had sided with the teachers during the strike) were opposed to my second term. Moreover, former Mayor Robert Wagner, who had entered the Democratic primary again, was seeking Liberal support—and he had won the endorsement of the party when he had last run for mayor in 1961. Just before the Liberal Party convention, a political reporter told an aide of mine, "Wagner wouldn't be running again if he didn't have the Liberal Party in his pocket."

As it turned out, the Liberals endorsed me, thus insuring that whatever happened in the Republican primary I would be on the ballot in November, and so would my running mates. We needed that support, because without it my candidacy would have been even more improbable on June 18.

On June 17 I lost the Republican primary to Senator

Marchi. The spread was about 6,000 votes out of some 200,000. I won Manhattan by almost three to one and lost every other borough, in spite of the support of the leadership of the organizations in Brooklyn and Queens.

But both of my running mates, Sandy Garelik and Fred Perrotta, won the GOP primary. This split created a situation in which the Republican-Conservative candidate for Mayor was supporting the Conservative Party candidates for City Council president and controller; the Liberal Party was running two Republicans and a Democrat; the Liberal-Independent Mayor was supporting two other men running on the Republican line; and the Republican organization found itself with a registered Democrat as its candidate for City Council president.

My own defeat at the polls was the first one I had ever taken in public life, and it stung. But my guess is that the people of New York, waking up to Wednesday morning's results, were more surprised than I was. First, I was not unprepared for defeat. My campaign manager, Dick Aurelio, and Alex Rose of the Liberal Party had predicted the loss privately to me. In fact, I had predicted it to myself. And, in terms of the fall race, there was suddenly a brand-new picture.

Among the Democrats, four moderates and liberals (including former Mayor Wagner) had split 68 per cent of the vote, leaving the winner, Mario Procaccino, the city controller, with 32 per cent of the vote. As the most conservative Democrat in the race, his pitch in the primary had been a straight "law and order" line. His one television commercial, shown over a picture of a burning building at the City University, was a not-so-subtle appeal to racial fear. "Discriminating quotas cannot be tolerated," the announcer said. "Mario Procaccino will represent *you* for a change."

Thus New York City found both major parties running conservative candidates for mayor. And in that situation, there was at least a chance that I could win. I have no idea whether I could have beaten any of the other Democratic candidates, but I do know that the results of the primary, in the perverse way that politics sometimes takes, aided my effort because it established a vitally important point in the minds of New Yorkers: that an election is not a referendum on an incumbent's popularity alone—it is also a measure of alternatives.

The day after the primary I held my first press conference and promptly made a mistake. That morning was a jumble of phone calls to Democrats, Republicans, and independents, asking them to hold some time for talks with me and telling them that we were trying to put a coalition together, that I was in the race to stay. Consequently, I took less time than usual for a discussion with my aides of what I wanted to say; and thus, the point I was trying to make about the need to turn away from the leadership of fear and conservatism came out distorted. The unintended implication of what I said was that New Yorkers who had chosen the primary winners were somehow racists and bigots, a statement neither politically smart nor in any way true on the merits. Particularly for an incumbent who had been thought of as aloof and arrogant, the sense that I could not tolerate people who disagreed with me was an inauspicious beginning to the general campaign.

There was, in any case, much work to be done. In the wake of Procaccino's victory, an enormous number of Democrats were searching for some alternative to his candidacy. There were, really, only two ways they could go—either support of a fourth candidate (Bronx Borough President Herman Badillo, Brooklyn Congressman Hugh Carey, or other such leaders), or join a coalition with me. It was thus our first post-primary effort to stop a fourth candidate, for another liberal candidate would almost certainly drain off enough liberal-moderate votes to guarantee Procaccino the election.

This effort was actually summer-long, because we could not know until the fall, when nominating petitions were due, whether we had succeeded in averting such a drive. It began immediately after the primary with the enlistment of West Side reform leader Ronnie Eldridge, who immediately opened the lines of contacts to Democrats all over the city. Within twenty-four hours after the primary, she had sparked an endorsement of me by some twenty prominent New Yorkers, including many former associates of the late Robert Kennedy, which explicitly warned against a fourth candidate.

The effort continued with a loose alliance with the New Democratic Coalition, a group which I almost bored to death in my first meeting with them but which I managed to begin communicating with the second time around. In mid-July the New Democratic Coalition endorsed my candidacy—and the beginnings of a coalition began to be seen. Further, many New York Republicans stayed with me after my defeat. Although Governor Rockefeller, and then President Nixon, announced their support of Senator Marchi, I retained the support of Senator Javits, Senator Goodell, the Manhattan county organization, Attorney General Lefkowitz, and a number of Republican state legislators (the number, I think, was two). Meanwhile, the state Republican organization, led by the state chairman, began closing the vise on every Republican in sight in order to block support for me—including financial support. Leading Republican fund raisers, however, long committed to the progressive wing of the party, stood firm for me. One of them, Gustav Levy, continued as my Finance Chairman, as he had been since the beginning of the campaign. In my twenty years of political experience, he is the best I have ever seen.

Throughout the summer we gained the endorsements of a string of Democrats. We had pledged to put together a Fusion Advisory Council composed of Democrats, Republicans, and Liberals to help chart election strategy. We kept this promise, and this council and I began meeting every week. Whatever disagreements opened up, the lines of contact were kept open—something which is owed in great measure to the patience and skill of my campaign manager, Richard Aurelio. One by one, Democrats began standing up to support me. Howard Samuels, Democratic candidate for lieutenant governor in 1966, was one of the first. Herman Badillo, who had run a strong race in the Democratic primary, was another. So was Brooklyn Congresswoman Shirley Chisholm.

These endorsements were an important part of our campaign strategy. No candidate and no organization can ever claim to see in advance exactly how a campaign should be charted; too many events intervene. But in this case, the steps we had agreed on at the beginning bore up suprisingly well throughout the campaign.

If there was one key decision we made early which proved to be right, it was the decision to go out into the neighborhoods of New York every day and night, confronting those who might well not vote for me. In an age of television, that kind of direct contact is often thought of as obsolete, but in New York a sense of helplessness was too great to be cured by using television alone. It was imperative for me to be seen, to talk with people on their turf, to listen to their grievances and answer them.

This required specific concentration on undecided neighborhoods in Brooklyn, the Bronx, and Queens. Mario Procaccino was running a campaign aimed squarely at the disaffections I have already summarized, calling me the candidate of the "Manhattan arrangement" (the wealthy, the businessmen, the communications media), charging that I had "sold out" to troublemakers and militants. In some parts of the city this charge had been accepted before Procaccino's campaign had even begun, and there was little I could do. But in other neighborhoods—the usually middle-class, traditionally liberal, and in great measure Jewish communities of New York—the feeling seemed to be disaffection with me combined with uncertainty about Democrat Procaccino. Indeed, very early in the campaign a general kind of statement in these undecided neighborhoods was taking shape: "Lindsay may be terrible, but look what they're giving us as an alternative." And it was into these neighborhoods that I went, night after night, to try to answer questions more than to make speeches.

We began this effort on Labor Day with a swing through the Bronx, Brooklyn, and Queens, stopping at beaches and swim clubs where crowds had gathered for the unofficial last weekend of the summer. It was the start of our effort to go directly into the neighborhoods we had to recapture to win the election.

The weekend was a completely incredible experience. I was cheered, booed, assaulted, complimented, sympathized with ("He looks so tired," I heard often—a bad sign for the first day of campaigning!), splashed, applauded, and heckled. I gave my first speech of the campaign to a crowd of faintly bemused swimmers, reporters, advance men, staff, and youthful hecklers. It looked a little ludicrous on the evening news, and I guess it *was* a little ludicrous to deliver a speech into the teeth of general clamor. But it had to be done, as proof that we were in fact running an open, visible campaign, taking on the tough political job of winning back former supporters and appearing and speaking in every part of the city.

This kind of direct confrontation can be an unsettling experience at times. New Yorkers, happily, hold to the sense that the Mayor is fully their equal, and that at the same time he bears direct responsibility for city dilemmas. Unlike presidents or governors, who are distant, the mayor is *there*—and even when a mayor's constituency is larger than that of almost every other governor of every other state, it is still him to whom New Yorkers turn, even for the most specific details about city issues.

I can remember, during one meeting in the Bronx, a man angrily getting to his feet to ask what appeared to be a question powered entirely by rage. "Mr. Mayor," he began angrily, "I want to know what are parking meters doing on Fordham Road?"

Or again, in Queens, a young man launched his question with an angry speech about inefficiency in sanitation services. "You're cheating on my neighborhood to serve someplace else in New York, and I say that's wasteful and dishonest. And by the way," he added, without changing his tone of voice, "I'm *for* you."

More important than the lighter moments were the serious issues where give-and-take proved vital. New Yorkers were concerned about crime, and rightly so. I tried to speak about the innovations we had made, about the launching of the fourth police platoon, about the police modernizations we had fought for and won. But what was really on their minds in many cases was the unasked questions. Was I handcuffing the police? Did I really try to curry favor with militants by buying them off? Was I attending to minority groups at their expense?

Few will actually ask these questions, so I tried, in my talks before the question period, to raise them myself—pleading guilty to the charge of concern about *all* of the city's minorities, the first *and* the last minorities; arguing that police were handcuffed not by a mayor but by outmoded procedures and insufficient resources to back up their work. Whether it worked, I don't know. But I do know that our decision to go into the neighborhoods of New York was no waste of time, either politically or in terms of what it taught me for a second term.

There was, of course, another way of reaching New Yorkers, and that was with television. I was lucky in this campaign to have Dave Garth, a consultant on communications who has been with me for five years, to direct our media campaign. He in turn had selected the advertising agency of Young & Rubicam to produce our commercials. Y&R's young president, Steve Frankfurt, and its creative chief, Tony Isadore, proved to have a real political sense. They understood that I was not a product, that a campaign was not an effort to sell toothpaste, and that the chief point of these commercials was to present my record in a way that went beyond laundry lists of achievements.

But what proved to be the key of our commercial campaign was a one-minute spot in which I talked both about the mistakes and the successes of the first four years. Far from being cynical, it was, I think, an important commercial beyond any possible political gain because it let New Yorkers know that their grievances *had* been heard, that their discontents *were* understood. The simple willingness to say "that was a mistake" had a kind of cleansing effect on much of the bitterness that had surfaced during the last years; it was a kind of signal that politicians were not beyond the reach of the people. And that was no mistake.

By September we had achieved one critical victory—there was no fourth candidate in the race. In that same month we received a major boost from totally unexpected quarters. I had called a conference of all New York's district attorneys to coordinate a narcotics drive, and after the conference Manhattan District Attorney Frank Hogan, a thirty-year veteran of the job and generally considered the best in the country at it, was asked a question about my record.

"I think," Hogan said, "that John Lindsay has done more for law enforcement than any mayor I know, and I go back to LaGuardia."

Hogan made clear that he was not offering a political endorsement ("I don't know how he is at cleaning up the snow," he added), but the impact of the words was overwhelming. Hogan is not a political figure; he is a registered Democrat who is totally dedicated to law enforcement. And those few words did far more than anything I could to undercut Procaccino and Marchi on the law-and-order issue. It meant that a professional crime fighter, speaking as such and not as a politician, recognized the value of the four-year fight we were waging. It was one thing for Procaccino to attack me; it was another for him to challenge the knowledge of District Attorney Hogan.

A wholly different event taking place during September and October also proved to be helpful, although I hesitate to invest it with the critical importance others have. The New York Mets, a baseball team often loved by New Yorkers not wisely but too well, began to make a serious run for the National League's Eastern Division title. Years ago we had gotten used to World Series and pennants, won each year by the Yankees, but since their decline no one really thought the Mets could follow in their footsteps. But suddenly the Mets began to look like a winning team—and New Yorkers began rooting for them like they had never rooted before. Now there were not three teams fighting for two pennants. There were the Mets.

Their astonishing victory—capped by both the pennant and the World Series—had an unbelievably tonic effect on the town. There was, for the first time in a long time, the sense that this city was on top again and that its people were not at each other's throats but were instead standing side by side rooting a New York team on.

There are those who think the most important thing that happened to me was getting doused with champagne in the Mets' dressing room after they had won the pennant and the World Series. I was, in all honesty, an innocent bystander, and reports that I supplied the champagne are not true. In fact, I had walked into the Mets dressing room to congratulate Gil Hodges and was standing well outside of the combat area when Rod Gaspar and Tom Seaver approached me with thoroughly malicious glints in their eyes. The next thing I knew, champagne was drenching me from my hair to my suit jacket. That is the whole story of a nonpolitical event. And if you don't believe me, you can ask Deputy Mayor Gil Hodges.

But I think a more significant event was the spontaneous victory celebration that erupted all over the city when the Mets won the Series. The confetti and paper that poured out of downtown and midtown offices (that the sanitation force—and I—spent all night cleaning up), the impromptu parades and motorcades, created a moment of pure joy in a city that doesn't often have these moments. And it did, I think, produce a sense of unity and satisfaction that made New Yorkers a little more reconciled to the ups and downs of their city.

Finally, as September passed into October, the continuing endorsements of Democrats became more and more important. Every day, New Yorkers picked up their papers to learn that another prominent Democrat was defecting from his party's choice to support me. What this meant was more than a list of names. It meant that in neighborhoods where I was viewed with suspicion, other people, with far closer ties to their communities, were willing to back me. Assemblyman Leonard Simon, for instance, put in long hours of campaigning with me and talking for me. Congressman Ben Rosenthal of Queens did the same. Writer Jimmy Breslin (who has already claimed his modest share of credit for my re-election) did make a difference, because he was far closer to the real New York than any politician. And Arthur Goldberg clearly made a real impact with his courageous, independent, and well-timed endorsement of me in mid-October.

Another key factor was the series of televised debates among the three candidates. Procaccino had sought to identify me as an "actor who went on TV and smiled while the city burned." Interestingly, there were many on my staff who thought Procaccino could win the debates simply by showing up and remaining calm, since his image as an emotional candidate had been exaggerated by the press.

We had made the decision early to discuss specific, concrete issues—police reorganization, rent control, tax reform, Vietnam, and some others—and avoid any personal clash with either opponent. This proved to be sound strategy, and when Procaccino began a string of last-minute charges, the effect was to confirm rather than rebut the "emotional-candidate" tag. And again, the opportunity for voters to make comparisons among the candidates clearly helped me in the last weeks of the campaign.

In the midst of Arthur Goldberg's endorsement and the Mets' drive to the series title, a far more somber event was taking shape—the October 15 Vietnam War Moratorium. Begun by the youthful leaders of Eugene McCarthy's student campaign, the one-day marking of the war had mushroomed into a national day of quiet recognition and protest of what the war had done to us as a people. It was unusual because it was centered in the cities and towns of America, at neighborhood levels of participation. And it was, probably, the most unusual such demonstration in American history.

I had months earlier determined to make Vietnam and the distorted national priorities a campaign issue. Part of the reason was obvious—services in New York were not at a fair level. Though taxes were higher, services were squeezed. I believed then (and still do) that the critical reason for this imbalance is the enormous drain on our resources produced by an $80 billion defense budget and by a $30 billion war in Vietnam we never should have fought. I had said over and over that New York City is a "prisoner of war," that its taxpayers contribute $9 billion each year to war and defense spending and that this money had to begin coming back to the city.

There was thus no doubt in my mind that I would personally participate in the moratorium. The question was what the city should do, if anything. Clearly, there was deep division over the war, and to enlist the city officially on the side of protest would cause great disagreement.

I decided finally to mark the day with a special note of somberness—the lowering of city flags and the decking of City Hall in mourning bunting. The purpose was to remind New Yorkers of the real cost of the war, beyond any measure of money—the deaths of thousands of our young men. It was supposed to be a measure of respect for those—particularly the families of those who had been killed—who still supported the struggle out of this kind of emotional tie. It turned out to be interpreted as a kind of political act (which may well have been inevitable) and produced great hostility among police and firemen in particular. But it was clear to me that it was essential to make some kind of gesture to remind New Yorkers of what the war had done to all of us. It was for that reason that the Proclamation the city produced was put in terms of a day of observance for the costs of the war on a personal, individual basis.

The lowering of the flags undoubtedly hurt me politically—our telephone canvass showed that during the next few days. But it is equally clear that, as a political matter, my strong stand in opposition to the war was a help. First, it hit hardest in precisely those communities where the undecided vote was greatest—the middle-class, educated neighborhoods. Second, as a purely political judgment, most people in New York, however they phrased it, desperately wanted the War in Vietnam ended and did not support the continued effort to fight a military battle there. Third, I think somehow my stand again forced New Yorkers to look to the alternatives—to see whether my opponents were willing to commit themselves on this issue. It reminded New Yorkers that we were linked to the rest of the country, and that a mayor unwilling to call for new national directions might be a mayor unwilling to recognize the real dilemma of the city.

Beyond any explicit issue in the campaign there were a host of intangibles. One of them had already been made clear before the election—a sense of personal antipathy to me. But as the campaign progressed, the intangible issues began to turn against Mario Procaccino.

There was his initial refusal to debate on television, which seemed to many an attempt to hide. There was the sense of confusion he often projected, particularly in talking with newsmen. There was his attempt to label a high-risk rehabilitation program as an effort to "buy off" troublemakers—which, I believe, backfired by raising some questions among key voting constituencies about the depth of his understanding about crime.

But most important, there began to develop sometime in October a sense that the city was not all that bad, that everything that happens is not the Mayor's fault, and that among the alternatives John Lindsay might not be so bad after all.

The most "tangible" intangible, I suppose, was the *Daily News* poll. First published three weeks before election, the poll showed me out in front by eleven points, and ultimately gave me a victory by twenty-one percentage points—a margin of some 600,000.

I should say at the outset that I did not believe the poll, because it simply did not square with any of our own samplings or my own sense of how the situation felt. We never had 49 per cent of the Bronx vote, and we never had 48 per cent of the Brooklyn vote. More interesting, I think, is that the *News* poll may have been one of the few polls which hurt *both* leading candidates at the same time.

It hurt Procaccino in obvious ways. Money dried up; his staff was surely demoralized; and Democrats wavering between endorsing him and neutrality, or between neutrality and endorsing me, were pushed in my direction by the poll.

But on Election Day, the *News* poll hurt me badly. For many New Yorkers, the decision had been to vote for me—very reluctantly. "I don't like Lindsay but we can't have Procaccino," the refrain most often went. But if the *News* poll was right, these New Yorkers could have it both ways—they could simply stay home and not vote at all, knowing that Procaccino would not win. In fact, so prevalent was this tendency in some neighborhoods that our own post-election sampling indicated that I had lost anywhere from 150,000 to 400,000 votes because the *News* poll had convinced reluctant Lindsay voters to stay home.

At midnight on November 4 at our headquarters, one of my assistants came up to shake my hand. "My deepest condolences," he said. It was an appropriate measure of our victory.

We had won—by about 185,000 votes and with 42 per cent of the vote. The results were hardly a cause for rejoicing—by any of us. Mario Procaccino and his supporters surveyed a Democratic Party in ruins, far less united than it was when I was first elected Mayor in a fusion campaign in 1965. Senator Marchi, in turn, had received the lowest vote of any Republican candidate for Mayor in forty years, lower even than in 1957, when Robert Christenberry ran what was regarded as the classic campaign designed not to win an election. In 1969 the Republican minority was even swept out of second place on the City Council, replaced by the Liberal Party as the number-two party in the Council.

Ironically, even some of the Republicans from conservative districts found themselves defeated by a Liberal

Party candidate. (Significantly, the Democratic candidate in Harlem, who was as far to the left as some of the most conservative Republicans were to the right, was also defeated by the Liberal Party candidate.)

As for myself, I had won without the support of either major party. But what I had won was a city that still was in desperate financial shape and whose people still were disaffected from the kind of lives they were leading. I had won because of a patient electorate, a great campaign staff, and hard work. But the kind of effort needed to govern the city was going to be a lot harder than winning an election. I now thought that I had one key advantage aside from a more sympathetic City Council and Board of Estimate—and that was the kind of thing I had learned from the campaign.

The first was a lesson about the new kind of disaffected American—the "silent majority" of which the President speaks, the white working or middle class, as they are sometimes called. For some, particularly some politicians, the middle-class mainstream American is fed up with efforts to win racial justice or economic opportunity and is determined to vote out political figures advocating that kind of effort. In my judgment, this is totally misleading. The mainstream American *is* aggrieved and often *does* protest social programs. But that protest arises less from a sense of innate conservatism than from a sense that his own, very real grievances are being neglected. Consider his own state for a moment.

In New York City he makes, on the average, about $8,000 a year, a sum that to a jobless ghetto youth seems a king's ransom. The Department of Labor, however, tells us that to live "moderately" in New York City a family of four needs an income of more than $9,500 a year. And thus, in the words of one national publication, he lives "in anxious suspension above poverty but well below affluence."

He is told that he is better off than ever before, and a glance at his paycheck proves that he earns more than ever before. But inflation has eaten away the value of his pay increases—inflation that has, since the outbreak of the War in Vietnam, tripled its pace. His taxes have risen swiftly, and so great has been this combined pressure of higher prices and higher taxes that the average worker's disposable real income has actually *declined* since 1965.

He sees on all sides not a steadily improving life but a steadily more pressurized existence. If he wants to move to a new home, it is all but impossible to find financing he can afford; yet if he waits, he sees the cost of new housing increase by some 7 per cent a year. He does not know how he will care for his family should any of them be sick because hospital costs in New York City *average* $60 a day, and most insurance plans do not cover anything like the full cost of an illness.

He knows that a college education for his children is critical if they are to have the chance to gain the genuinely affluent life he wants them to have. But if he has two children he knows that sending them to college will cost three years of his *total income,* and that cost is going to rise far faster than his income in the next few years.

He sees his taxes rising—or at least taking a larger chunk out of every additional dollar he earns in pay increases. But, particularly if he lives in a big city, his services have been starved for funds for decades, and thus the streets are not clean enough, there is too much crime, too much pollution, too much inconvenience in travel—and he wonders what he is paying all this money for.

It is this kind of disaffection, I think, that formed the backdrop for what others have cited as a reactionary tendency. Because, in addition to all these unresolved problems, the mainstream American is also afflicted with the overwhelming malaise of modern America—the loss of the sense of individual autonomy. For a middle-class resident of New York, talking to the government is an exercise in futility, as it is in most instances for any individual dealing with any enormous bureaucracy. There is no sense that anyone is listening, no sense that anyone in power has even a measure of the problem, much less a program for changing these conditions.

And it is exactly here that the sense of resentment is born. For in the last few years, governments at all levels have mounted a wide range of programs to aid the deprived. They have in the main been meager programs; they have in no sense represented the commitment of resources and energy we need—but they *have* been visible. Many governments, New York City's included, have attempted to break through the decades of neglect and demonstrate to our most deprived citizens that the government cares about them and that through such devices as the Urban Action Task Force it can respond to their grievances.

And seeing this—seeing at least effort and concern among one part of the citizenry—the mainstream New Yorker may well ask: "Where is an effort being made to answer *my* grievances? Is the black man to be bettered at my expense?" And thus he may look on efforts to expand college admissions as threats to his child's place at the free-tuition City University; he may see efforts to increase job opportunities as threats to his own job; he may see his own far-from-secure foothold endangered by the progress of other groups.

It was and is this kind of disaffection that must be met, in New York and in other cities. And the way to do it is with programs that protect this New Yorker—in education for his children, services in his neighborhood, and an increased share of participation for his neighborhood, too. It *can't* be done by cutting back on programs designed to help the man who is in even more trouble than he is.

Another key element in this drive is the welding of a coalition of cities speaking for both the poor and the mainstream American, to fight for the kinds of changes that can better his life—not only federal programs, but tax reform, university education for his children that he can afford, and the chance to feel as though the forces that govern him are still within his control.

These are some of the challenges I faced as I prepared to start my second term. But there was also four years of experience to draw on. Those experiences—and what they taught me—is what the rest of this book is about. I have not touched on all of the vital issues affecting New York—housing, health, education, environment; that would require a dozen such books. But I have tried in what follows to suggest the dimensions of the city's struggle for survival—and the urgency of action to win that struggle.

II

The Root of the City's Ills

IN ONE SENSE, we can trace all the problems of the American city back to a single starting point: we Americans don't like our cities very much.

That is, on the face of it, absurd. After all, more than three-fourths of us now live in cities, and more are flocking to them each year. We are told that the problems of our cities are receiving more attention in Washington, and scholarship has discovered a whole new field to master and doctor in urban studies.

Nonetheless, it is historically true: in the American psychology, the city has been a basically suspect institution, reeking of the corruption of Europe, totally lacking that sense of spaciousness and innocence of the frontier and the rural landscape.

I don't pretend to be a scholar on the history of the city in American life. But my thirteen years in public office, first as an officer of the U.S. Department of Justice, then as Congressman, and now as Mayor of the biggest city in America, have taught me all too well the fact that a strong anti-urban attitude runs consistently through the mainstream of American thinking. Much of the drive behind the settlement of America was in reaction to the conditions in European industrial centers—and much of the rhetoric behind the basis of freedom in America was linked directly to the availability of land and the perfectibility of man outside the corrupt impulses of the city.

What has this to do with the predicament of the modern city? I think it has much to do with it. For the fact is that the United States, particularly the federal government, which has historically established our national priorities, has simply never really thought that the American city was "worthy" of improvement—at least not to the extent of expending any basic resources on it.

As a center of unhealthy, immoral, and depraved citizens, the city has seemed to many of our important and revered thinkers a condition to be avoided, not a problem to be solved. And it is also a fact that we *do* make public policy out of private prejudices, particularly when such prejudices run through the mainstream of American thought. What I suggest, then, is that at least part of the dilemma we find ourselves in is a product of a long heritage that has taught us to divorce the city from the purpose and hopes of the American experience. I think, too, that as we look at what has happened to the twentieth-century American city, we will see the shaping impulses of eighteenth- and nineteenth-century thinking on what did—and did not—happen.

Antipathy to the city predates the American experience. When industrialization drove the European working man into the major cities of that continent, books and pamphlets appeared attacking the city as a source of crime, corruption, filth, disease, vice, licentiousness, subversion, and high prices. The theme of some of the earliest English novels—*Moll Flanders* abounds in it—is that of the innocent country youth coming to the big city and being subjected to all forms of horror until justice—and a return to the pastoral life—follow.

The proper opinion of Europe seemed to support the Frenchman who wrote: "In the country, a man's mind is free and easy, and at his own disposal; but in the city, the persons of friends and acquaintances, one's own and other people's business, foolish quarrels, ceremonies, visits, impertinent discourses, and a thousand other fopperies and diversions steal away the greatest part of our time and leave no leisure for better and necessary employment. Great towns are but a larger sort of prison to the soul, like cages to birds or pounds to beasts."

This was not, of course, the only opinion on city life. Others maintained that the city was "the fireplace of civilization, whence light and heat radiated out into the cold dark world." And William Penn planned Philadelphia as "the holy city," carefully laid out so that each house would have the appearence of a country cottage to avoid the density and overcrowding that so characterized European cities.

Without question, however, the first major thinker to express a clear antipathy to the urban way of life was Thomas Jefferson. For Jefferson, the political despotism of Europe and the economic despotism of great concentrations of property and wealth, on the one hand, and poverty and deprivation, on the other, were symbolized by the cities of London and Paris, which he visited frequently during his years as a diplomatic representative of the new nation. In the new world, with its opportunities for widespread landholding, there was the chance for a flowering of authentic freedom, with each citizen, freed from economic servility, both able and eager to participate in charting the course of his own future. America, in a real sense, was an escape from all the injustice that had flourished in Europe—injustice that crystallized in the big city.

This belief of Jefferson's was pervasive. "I think our governments will remain virtuous for centuries," he wrote James Madison in 1787, "as long as they are chiefly agricultural, and this will continue as long as there shall be vacant lands in any part of America. When they get piled upon one another, in large cities, as in Europe, they will become corrupt as in Europe."

And writing to the noted medical figure Benjamin Rush in 1800 concerning an outbreak of yellow fever, he said: "When great evils happen, I am in the habit of looking out for what good may arise from them as consolations to us. . . . The yellow fever will discourage the growth of great cities in our nation, and I view great cities as pestilential to the morals, the health, and the liberties of man. True, they nourish some of the elegant arts, but the useful ones can thrive elsewhere, and less perfection in the others, with more health, virtue, and freedom, would be my choice."

In 1807, asking a colleague in Philadelphia to care for his grandson, who was about to begin his medical education there, he apologized for sending his progeny in to the city: "I am not a friend," he said, "to placing young men in populous cities, because they acquire there habits and partialities which do not contribute to the happiness of their after life."

This Jeffersonian theme was to remain an integral part of American tradition. Throughout the nineteenth century, as the explorations of America pushed farther outward, the new settlers sounded most like each other in their common celebration of freedom from city chains.

These views of the city as inimical to all the virtues of wisdom, morality, liberty, and decency are by no means isolated. They are persistent themes of the nineteenth century. They are reflected by observers such as de Tocqueville, in his classic *Democracy in America,* published in 1839, when he observed: "To subject the provinces to the metropolis . . . is not only to place the destiny of the empire in the hands of a portion of the community, which may be . . . unjust, but to place it in the hands of a populace acting under its own impulses, which must be avoided as dangerous. . . . I look upon the size of certain American cities, and especially on the nature of their population, as a real danger which threatens the future security of the New World."

We find this belief, too, reflected by less noted commentators such as this one, writing in *The Prairie Farmer* of 1849: "The pursuits of agriculture . . . are connected with everything around us which tends to enlighten and ennoble the mind, improve the condition of society, and promote the common welfare. . . . The 'poetry' of city life . . . crushes, enslaves, and ruins so many thousands of our young men, who are insensibly made the victims of dissipation, of reckless speculation, and of ultimate crime."

Or this comment, from the same publication a year later (1850): "Those of the city (at least many of them) have no steady habit of a virtuous tendency, and consequently acquire habits of an immoral nature instead of cultivating such noble and refined sentiments as are induced from rural employments."

We even find the first hints that those who inhabit the cities are somehow less "American" than their rural counterparts. The suspicion arose early in America—an Ohio settler wrote, in 1815, that insulation from the "foreign commerce" which touched the life of the eastern city would help insure that the citizens of Ohio would be "more patriotic."

The point is that all this opinion goes beyond ill feeling; it suggests a strong national sense that encouragement and development of the city was to be in no sense a national priority—that our manifest destiny lay in the untouched lands to the west, in constant movement westward, and in maximum dispersion of land to as many people as possible.

In fact, that was national policy, reflected in most of our important laws. While federal influence was extended into that one aspect of city life that was deemed important to the nation at large—development of port and navigation facilities to expedite trade—the impulse of the country was toward expansion rather than an effort to ameliorate conditions in the big city.

Thus, the Northwest Ordinance of 1787—perhaps the first important declaration of national policy—explicitly encouraged migration into the Northwest Territory and provided grants of land and free public lands for schools. New York City, by contrast, did not begin a public-education system until 1842—and received, of course, no federal help at all. Similarly, the Homestead Act of 1862 was based on an assumption—supported by generations of American theory—that in the West could be found genuine opportunity and that the eastern-seaboard cities of the United States were simply hopeless conglomerations of vice and deprivation.

This belief accelerated after the Civil War, for a variety of reasons. For one thing, the first waves of immigration were being felt around the country, and the economically deprived conditions of the immigrants, largely from Ireland and Northern Europe, caused many in rural America to identify economic want with personal inferiority—a trend that has not exactly disappeared from our national thinking. Attacks on the un-American and criminal tendencies of the Irish, the Slavs, and every other ethnic group that arrived on America's shores were a steady part of national thinking, as were persistent efforts to bar any further migration of "undesirables" to our country.

Accompanying this trend was the start of important attacks on the whole economic structure of the American economy—a structure in which concentration of wealth and poverty were both identified as evils associated with the big city. We see this kind of thinking even in optimistic works about the city. Thus, writing of western cities at the start of the 1860's, Jessup Scott predicted happily: "A large influx of these laborers, though it may lower the average character of our people, will, it is hoped, in a greater degree, elevate theirs."

Writing of the signs of the "Gilded Age" in San Francisco at the middle of the nineteenth century, William Kelly said: "In San Francisco nothing is natural—everything is forced; it is a hotbed where all pursuits are stimulated by the fierce fire of one predominant lust. Trade or business is not embarked on there to be the honorable occupation of a lifetime; professions are not solely followed to secure a permanent practice and social elevation; men engage in both one and the other to build up fortunes in a hurry with whatever materials they can grasp, to win a large stake by any means and then withdraw . . . until conscience is left without a corner to hide in, and even common decency is obliged to pick her steps through the mire."

By 1857 the first attacks on the other end of the economic scale were being heard across the continent, and while the impulse clearly was toward reform, the image of the American city as a place of indecency was again being reinforced. In the report of a New York legislative committee "Appointed to Examine Into the Condition of Tenant Houses in New York and Brooklyn," the investigators reported: "Here, in sad refutation of utopian speculation, the leper crouches in dumb despair, the beggar crawls in abject misery, the toiler starves, the robber prowls, and the tenant-house—home of all those outcast human beings—rises in squalid deformity, to mock civilization with its foul malaria, its poison-breeding influences, its death-dealing associations."

With the coming of rapid industrialization, all the results of investigations into city poverty and despair that we think of as recent findings were being reported—and each report served to confirm the beliefs of the Founding Fathers that the city was no place for a respectable American. Indeed, this opinion grew. We find evidence of it in 1890, when, at the New York constitutional convention, a delegate defended malapportionment on the ground that since the rural communities of New York were wiser, more virtuous, and more moral than the decadent city, their residents *should* receive disproportionate weight.

Whatever the speaking ability of this delegate, his point was picked up and endorsed all over the country. It is safe to say that in the years of maximum population growth of the cities—between 1890 and 1950—not a single city in the United States was fairly represented either in state legislatures or in the House of Representatives. (Since state legislatures draw the congressional boundaries, it is easy to see why a malapportioned state legislature slanted in favor of rural areas would draw congressional boundaries that favored rural areas.)

Now consider carefully what this meant. This sixty-year period was the time when basic social legislation was being shaped in every state legislature and in the Congress. It was the period during which the basic taxation policy of state and local governments was set down in New York; the first basic commitment was made by state and local governments to various social and economic policies such as unemployment insurance, workmen's compensation, and home relief; and the first fundamentally important steps were taken in the structuring of state aid to localities, including aid to education. And it included the two great eras of federal activism in social concerns—the Progressive Era and the New Deal.

Thus, in all that time, the cities of America were never given their proportional voice in the halls of legislative deliberation, and all the fundamental charters of priority were set up without their full participation. And the laws showed it. Educational-aid formulas, for example, were carefully written so that big cities gained no advantage from the size of their populations, and in fact *lost* aid because of the very fact that they were contributing most heavily to teach their own children. The same laws initiated, at least in New York, the tradition of taking from the city far more than the state returned, and even of recognizing the necessity of losing some money to pay for state administrative costs.

Is all this relevant only to past attitudes and past legislative history? I don't think so. The fact is that until today, this same basic belief—that our cities ought to be left to fend for themselves—is still a powerful element in our national tradition.

Consider more modern history. The most important housing act in the last twenty-five years was not the statute that provided for public housing; it was the statute that permitted the FHA to grant subsidized low-interest mortgages to Americans who want to purchase homes. More than anything else, this has made the suburban dream a reality. It has brought the vision of grass and trees and a place to play for the kids within the reach of millions of working Americans, and the consequences be damned. The impact of such legislation on the cities was not even considered—nor was the concept of making subsidized money available for neighborhood renovation in the city so that it might compete with the suburban pitch. Instead, in little more than a decade 800,000 white middle-income New Yorkers fled the city for the suburbs and were replaced by largely unskilled nonwhites who in many instances represented a further cost rather than an economic asset.

Consider, too, the National Defense Highways Act (that name, by the way, graphically reveals the mentality of the 1950's, when a bill could not be passed if it did not include "defense" somewhere in its title). Under this bill, the United States committed itself to building an interstate highway system, ostensibly to insure that people and missiles could be moved effectively in case of nuclear attack. In fact, the bill was a $60 billion program for building highways, predominantly between the inner city and suburban communities and largely at the expense of inner-city neighborhoods. More than a dozen years have passed since this bill became law and we still do not have a federal trust fund that offers significant federal financing for mass transit.

And it was not a hundred years ago but two years ago that a bill appropriating a small amount of federal money for rat control was literally laughed off the floor of the House of Representatives amid much levity about discrimination against country rats in favor of city rats.

What happened, I think, was not the direct result of a "the city is evil and therefore we will not help it" concept. It was more indirect, more subtle, the result of the kind of thinking that enabled us to spend billions of dollars in subsidies ostensibly to preserve the family farm while doing nothing about an effective program for jobs in the city; to recognize agriculture, veterans, small business, labor, commerce, and the American Indian as legitimate interests but create no Department of Urban Development until 1965; to so restrict money that meaningful federal aid is still not feasible.

In other words, I believe that through a subtle link, the world of urban America as a dark and desolate place undeserving of support or help has become fixed in the American consciousness. And we are paying for that attitude in our cities today.

III

A Day in the Life

THE MAYOR OF NEW YORK presides over a city of 8 million people. During the working hours that population swells by several million people and tens of thousands of cars as the suburbanites flock to the core of Manhattan to work and shop and play. He presides over a city budget of $6.6 billion—greater than the budget of any single state. His city builds almost $2 billion a year in facilities. It employs 350,000 people. It teaches a million elementary and secondary school pupils every day. It puts 32,000 policemen on its streets each day to help protect safety. It tows away 100,000 illegally parked cars a year from midtown Manhattan alone, and hauls away 60,000 more cars that have simply been abandoned by their owners. It runs a court system that rivals that of any state.

The numbers are staggering. Each of them, in one way or another, touches my life every day. Each of them defines a small part of the job that a Mayor of New York has; each of them poses new demands on an overtaxed, undernourished city treasury; each of them demands more productivity from a governmental structure that can barely keep pace with outmoded definitions of its job.

For beyond these numbers are the cold, hard facts of city life. With such an enormous number of people, with such a disparate collection of facilities, a statistically small fraction can mean tremendous burdens. Of 8 million people, a certain percentage get sick every day, and some of them cannot afford their own medical care. That means a system of twenty municipal hospitals employing thousands of doctors and nurses who must care for numbers far greater than the system's capacity for proper treatment because it lacks funds.

A small portion of a $2 billion capital construction budget is inevitably going to be delayed. What that means is that in some neighborhoods important facilities are behind schedule, and a community is up in arms because something it needs is not ready.

On any given day some of the thousands of miles of road will be in disrepair—but in a city as densely populated and traffic-choked as New York the closing of a single lane of traffic on a single midtown street can snarl traffic for hours and send new waves of frustration coursing through the veins of the city.

In New York, in other words, every problem—even those that are statistically small—are large. And in cases where the problems are relatively large—such as in the achievement levels of city schoolchildren or the number of people on welfare—you have a crisis of major proportions on your hands.

Then, too, you begin to recognize what may be the prime fact of municipal life—the essential interdependency of problems and solutions.

Take air pollution. That seems like a simple, single problem: pass stiff legislation to put polluters out of business. Force them to improve their machinery or shut down. But it isn't that simple.

Every time you shut down an incinerator, you increase the amount of garbage on the city streets. Every time you do that, you either have to put more street-cleaning forces out or face the fact that you are going to have a dirtier city. If incinerators can't burn garbage, it's going to be put out on the street to be collected—or not collected. And that means that we are going to have to find the money to collect that garbage and to dispose of it rapidly, assuming we can find a place to bury it, before it builds up to the point where it engulfs us completely. So you cannot solve the pollution problem without solving the sanitation problem, and you can't solve either problem without money.

Or take traffic congestion. For years, people have been urging New York City to shut midtown Manhattan to private automobiles, which clog the streets and make midtown passage a challenge for Ulysses. But you cannot shut Manhattan to cars unless you are sure you are providing alternative transportation. That means mass transit—even more than we are now planning and engineering—from outlying areas into Manhattan, the core business and shopping district of the city.

Further, before you ban cars from midtown, you must listen to the arguments of the handicapped, United Nations diplomats and foreign consuls, garage operators, commuting businessmen, department store owners, merchants of every variety, the Automobile Association of America, and other powerful interests. And if you are not positive that you have designed an alternative to autos that works, you have lost not only an argument but also some of your credibility, without which any further attempt at city planning becomes virtually a lost cause. Thus the act of banning autos from midtown Manhattan is far from a unitary act of planning. It raises a wide range of other political, economic, and planning questions that are difficult to answer.

These are the kinds of question the Mayor is asked regularly. Because of the sheer size of the city and its government, almost every day brings with it basic planning decisions—decisions that will set the course of the city for years to come. If you approve a transit route, the location of a new industrial park, or a major housing project, you are committing great sums of money and great amounts of time on a single project that in turn will affect the entire life style of the surrounding area. And the city is so big that these decisions, which the Mayor of an average city may have to make once or twice in his term, are made by the Mayor of New York daily. Projects that would completely dominate the attention of most other towns are all but lost in the sheer enormousness of New York.

The only effective way I know to meet this problem is to get as much information as possible—information, and more information—and getting it determines much of my life. A typical day usually begins well before 8:00 A.M. on the telephone, an instrument that is a critical part of my life. Until well past midnight I am asking questions and answering them, listening to people and talking to them, on the phone or face to face, in an effort to know as much as possible about the consequences of each decision I must make.

Twice a week I meet with the principal policy makers of the city, the commissioners and administrators of the city departments and agencies. It is their prime responsibility to keep the basic city machinery running well and to design machinery to help it run better.

The City Planning Commission, for example, should know what the Economic Development Administration thinks about a proposed new city park site. Might it affect a decision of a major business firm to locate here? If so, are there alternative sites for a park? What is the increased cost of that alternative, and does the Budget Bureau think the greater costs are merited? Or should we risk losing a business that may move to the city because of the social benefit of that park at that time?

What is happening with the Regional Manpower Centers, designed to train and equip people with job skills? Are the centers behind schedule? If so, why? Are we lagging on capital-construction projects in this field, and if so is there anything we can do about it? Is the relevant agency hiring teachers and renting classroom space? If not, is it a lack of money? Is the Budget Bureau slowing down the program? If so, why?

By the time such a meeting is over the backlog of calls has already mounted. A call to Washington to an official in the Health, Education, and Welfare Department. For the fourth time, I argue for a total scrapping of the welfare system and a wholesale replacement by a federally funded program emphasizing job placement and advancement. A check with our Washington office to see whether or not the national administration has changed its mind on the proposal, and a reminder to find out when the funds that we were promised under the Housing Act will actually be reserved for us so we can start in with construction of low-income housing. A call from the leader of a public employees' union to tell me that a new vacation policy of a city department is in violation of a collective-bargaining provision and may trigger a strike. A call from a high school principal advising us of disorder in his school, coupled with a request for more police protection. A call from our Albany office to warn me that a bill is pending that will "mandate" certain unwanted costs on the city and its already bursting budget.

While all this is going on a community group may be waiting in another room in City Hall for a long-promised meeting. As I have already mentioned, almost every group in the city at one point or another wants to meet with the Mayor, because he is the highest elected official of the most immediate form of government. The problem is that the answers I give to their legitimate questions cannot, by definition, be satisfactory, unless the demand is for a specific, relatively low-cost request like a traffic light outside a school or the acceleration of an already-approved project.

Usually, however, the complaints are about more basic problems in the city. We don't have enough police. The garbage isn't picked up frequently enough. The subway system is a disgrace (in fact, the city does not even have authority over the subway system—it's the province of a state agency, the Metropolitan Transit Authority).

I listen to their inquiries and answer them the best way I can. But it won't do to say that every neighborhood wants more police—the questioner doesn't live in "every neighborhood," he lives in *this* neighborhood, and he does not want danger on *his* streets.

In late morning I may be meeting with any one of my assistants who are responsible for specific areas of city government—poverty, housing, environmental protection, sanitation. Such meetings are necessary to bring me up to date on developments within that agency: on programs that are or are not working well, on conflicts between the agency and other forces, either inside or outside of city government. If a crisis is serious enough, it may mean forty-five minutes of hastily called meetings or phone calls, throwing me further behind schedule.

Meanwhile, the calls keep coming. The director of our Washington office calls about the status of a program and wants me to call a Cabinet officer or a member of the Congress. A state senator or city councilman asks about a specific problem in his district. The Press Secretary has an inquiry from a newspaper that requires a fast answer about a politically sensitive subject. Someone from Albany says that the state legislature wants to know more about a tax-reform bill before taking action.

Or, if there is a scheduled press conference—generally, I have two a week—Tom Morgan, my Press Secretary, will meet with me and a small staff for the briefing. Here we'll try to plan our message and map out in advance a strategy for avoiding political traps that an innocent-looking press conference can produce. Finally, you must rely on your wits, and those of a good press secretary, to protect yourself from the dangers of a press conference: making policy through carelessly thought-out answers, giving off-the-cuff responses to unanticipated questions. So the press briefing may last a full hour to cover in advance as many questions as possible, straight or curved.

On any given day chances are I will give a talk somewhere at lunchtime (dinnertime as well). It may be the Queens-Brooklyn Rotary club, which wants specific problems about their region solved (What about the master plan for economic development of Jamaica? What is your proposal to reduce the welfare burden on New York?). It may be a conference on an issue directly affecting New York, such as pollution control or addiction. Speeches like these give me a chance to measure some of our progress. Four years ago I was talking about problems—today I am talking more about solutions.

After lunch, which is often a sandwich at my desk or in the car, I may go up to Gracie Mansion and spend the rest of the day working there. City Hall has been correctly labeled a gold-fish bowl, and there is no such thing as a private meeting. Any visitor is duly noticed by the press and accosted for comment on the way in or out. Gracie Mansion offers a far greater degree of privacy. It's also a less prepossessing, more comfortable place that City Hall, and meetings tend to be more congenial, as a general rule.

If it's time to plan the city's budget, I will be spending several days with officials from the Budget Bureau and city agencies going over our budget requests for each department. Budget time is probably the roughest time of all for me. I spend much of my day during this period in the office of the Budget Director, Fred Hayes, where budget teams are available and where there is less pressure from the phone. Coffee is consumed by the gallon. No other process demonstrates more graphically what is meant by the city's chronic shortage of money. To someone looking at a city budget, a $6.6 billion municipal budget seems insanely high. How could any budget request not be met? In a city of 8 million people the answer to that question is all too simple: our expenses keep going up far faster than our revenues, because the sources from which we get our money are basically stagnant. They do not grow with a growing economy.

At budget-setting time we receive and review agency requests. How much is this new program going to cost? What specifically will the social costs be if we do not adopt this program? If this program of medical services is not adopted, where is the impact likely to be felt? Increased hospitals costs for certain communities? If it's an addiction center that can't be funded, what does it tell us about the potential crime rate, and doesn't that justify the cost? How many housing units must be scrapped? How many summer jobs for high school students will we have to cut back on? These are the kinds of questions no Mayor wants to answer, for the choices are always impossible. But that is what it means to be Mayor at its most frustrating moments, for you choose not between two grandiose programs but between two essential services, attempting to figure out how best to distribute the thin resources that are available. Moreover, you do it knowing with dead certainty that next year at this same time you will be going through the same process—except worse—again, unless the Congress and state governments begin to recognize the full dimensions of city needs that have gone unmet.

After the budget retreat (or rout, as it sometimes has been), other specific problems may arise—frequently only in passing, since there is never enough time for commissioners, administrators, staff assistants, and others to schedule formal meetings. It may be that a conflict of judgment between two forces has arisen that I must resolve. It may be that an outside source is willing to underwrite the cost of a private program of help to the city, if we can convince that source of its importance. At any event, it means more time on the telephone.

By late afternoon the tempo has reached its peak (particularly if some important decision has made news, which is often). It reflects the simple fact that each decision the city makes sets in motion a series of other decisions—and for each of these there must be consultations with different city agencies, discussions with city groups that may be affected, and an attempt to find out whether that decision has proved to be the right one.

For example, we were battling last year for the passage of a bill in the state legislature to enable us to put another platoon of policemen on the city streets. As part of the state's domination of city government, the state had enacted a law telling the city when and how to deploy its own police forces, which are funded by the city and its taxpayers. Several times before the vote I had been on the telephone and held meetings concerning this issue with editorialists on New York newspapers and with key state legislators who were helping to push the bill through. Finally the fight was won, but then it was vital to put the change through with a minimum of dispute. This meant a series of talks with the Police Commissioner to discuss his plans for implementing the fourth platoon and our efforts to deal with the lawsuit the Patrolmen's Benevolent Association was instituting to invalidate the new law.

It meant talks between the Corporation Counsel and the Commissioner to buttress the legal case against the suit. It meant a short call to the president of the PBA to tell him that if we won the fight we would work with him and the Association to minimize any hardships that might arise from the new law. And it meant initial planning to decide when the fourth platoon would begin, and where—and what kind of criteria we would use to judge the effectiveness of putting a substantially greater number of men on the streets at night.

Then, before the afternoon ends, there may be a meeting of the Executive Committee of the Urban Coalition, or possibly a meeting with the U.S. Ambassador to the United Nations and our new UN Advisory Committee, designed to make New York a better host city to the hundreds of UN families in our midst.

It's a constant battle to try to hold dinnertime for my wife and children, and I'm successful only about once or twice a week, usually on the weekend. Given the realities of public life in New York, I am out almost every night making speaking engagements or attending meetings to drum up support for such major programs as summer youth recreational and employment programs, which depend on the willingness of those in the private sector to shoulder their burden. But at the infrequent family dinner I try to spend the time on strictly family matters. It usually doesn't work out that way. At some point during the meal a phone call will require an instant decision: delegating authority to make an on-the-spot decision on a specific city project, getting information about a suddenly erupting crisis, or just catching up on the phone calls that did not get completed during the day. More often, I work straight through until 10 or 11 and then have dinner on a tray near the phone in the library of Gracie Mansion. My wife had a warmer installed in the kitchen of the Mansion that works remarkably well, and can keep a cooked dinner fresh all night (it's too bad they can't do the same for a Mayor). Often Mary will join me while I eat, working on her own mountain of mail.

On the rare occasions that I am home with Mary and the children for dinner, I'm usually off afterward to whatever meeting has been arranged by me and my staff for that evening. As often as not, the schedule during the day has become so tight that I'm forced to hold some appointments in the car while traveling from Gracie Mansion to a speaking engagement and back. It's not a satisfactory way of doing business, particularly if five people are wedged into the back seats, but it is frequently the only alternative to putting off appointments indefinitely—and where a decision is required, there is no real choice. The city moves too fast to stop.

There is, you may have noticed, only one flaw in this tightly packed schedule. It leaves me almost no room for thinking. There are those, I know, who don't believe it is part of an executive's job to think: he is just supposed to decide by listening to all the options and checking one of three boxes. I can't work that way. Possibly because of a law-school background, I try to read the documents involved with a basic policy decision. And that means that I'm usually up until 1:00 A.M. and beyond.

There is, further, one part of a Mayor's job that cannot be scheduled. And that is the possibility of a crisis—a sudden interruption of normality by an unpredictable event. During the teachers' strike in New York City the desperate search for a solution brought my involvement in most other phases of city government virtually to a standstill. During threats of disorder over the first three summers of my administration there were long, unscheduled hours devoted to personal walks on the city streets and constant efforts to follow up on promises to open up communications between tense communities and the city.

But somehow, even when the crises come, the city still keeps running. It makes you wonder sometimes about all the effort you put in during the normal days, even with full knowledge that "normal" is far from good enough.

This, at any event, is a general picture of the way I spend my time. But the more important question is the goal of this effort. What is it we are trying to do in New York City?

I can briefly answer that question. We're trying to hold this city together against the forces that are steadily eating away at it. We're trying to keep it together and at the same time we're hoping to change it in fundamental ways. To better understand this job, it's probably necessary to examine the state of New York City as it had become before I took office, and to recognize why we felt the new administration would face an enormous burden.

IV

What We Found

ON JANUARY 1, 1966, I walked into City Hall for the first time as Mayor. It was a serene day—at least it was quiet, because a transit strike had shut down the buses and subways of the city. Walking into the Mayor's office to confront an honest-to-God crisis on my first day in office, I found a completely barren desk. Not a pencil, not a pad of paper, was left. And the telephone communications system between the Mayor and the city departments consisted of a single two-button telephone. At a time when instant access was critical, there was no direct line between the Mayor and Police or Fire or Traffic.

This has at times seemed to me a metaphor for the state of New York City as we found it in 1966.

No administration, however dedicated and capable, could have prevented the difficulties that afflicted New York, or any other city, in the late 1950's and 1960's. Too little money, too many demands, too many problems—these conditions would spell trouble for the best of governments. In New York, as in almost every major city in the country, these conditions had been stretched to the breaking point by a thirty-year record of substantial neglect, neglect so pervasive that my first impulse on taking office was to file suit to invalidate my election.

Put generally, not since the days of LaGuardia had the city administration really looked at the way city government was working. In 1961 there had been a major reform of New York's charter, which greatly increased the authority of the Mayor, but the problem was that while the charter had been reformed, the structure of the city government had not. The city was regarded as a collection of separate, disparate interest groups, each of which had nothing to do with the others. The goal was to keep the city afloat by ministering first to one group, satisfying it, and then turning to the next group whose dissatisfaction was at the crisis stage. By the early 60's, at least, the trap was complete—any other way of operation, any real change in the functioning of city government, would jeopardize the jerry-built stability of the balancing act. New York City was something like a circus performer walking a tightrope and juggling at the same time. Eventually it reached a point where the city was trapped out on the tightrope, on one foot. It could barely maintain its position, but any movement would tip the whole balance.

In these circumstances it is not surprising that many basic city programs and operations had never undergone any real examination to see if they were working. One of the great myths about city government is that the "old pros," the organization party regulars and the patronage seekers, were skillful, adept managers of city affairs.

Consider some of these findings:

• The Parks Department had no map showing its facilities citywide. To find out where a park was, one had to look it up separately from every other park. Thus, attempts to design an integrated system of park maintenance were all but doomed—it was like a road map where no two cities appeared on the same page.

• The Sanitation Department manufactured its own batteries at a cost several times higher than the market price. Why? Because nobody had ever asked why the Sanitation Department didn't buy the batteries instead of making them, and because any suggestion to shut down an inefficient government activity is regarded as sacrilegious by many, and in any event can easily bring on a strike.

• The city owned its own asphalt plants, no doubt because years earlier, either through scandal, cost, or tradition, it was considered an essential aspect of city government. By 1966 the cost was far higher than private purchase.

• The Mayor and the Transit Authority had experimented with air-conditioned subway cars in 1958; the cars had not worked, and the matter had been dropped. Nobody pursued it with any vigor, asking companies if new technological breakthroughs had made air-conditioning more feasible so that the millions of people who rode subways every day would not have to be subjected to the fifth circle of hell each time they did.

These instances are not isolated examples of inefficiency. They are symbols of management that did not manage, that did not plan, that simply did not recognize the slow, steady deterioration of services despite the steadily rising costs. This posed, to be frank, political problems for my administration. To change long-entrenched policy meant taking on long, debilitating fights within bureaucracies, which are not generally responsive to calls for swift and sudden change. Moreover, a changeover inevitably means mistakes, false starts, and union trouble; it inevitably means that the full depth of a problem is going to come to the surface; it inevitably means that demands for action will be linked back to *your* promises and *your* recognition that serious problems existed. But on this matter there was no choice, either politically or managerially. The heat simply had to be taken; otherwise conditions would have become intolerable. Further, we believed that there were changes that could be made which would give us a better shot at remedying the conditions afflicting the city.

Before we did so, however, we had to understand the depth of the problems. And that was unsettling, to say the least. Consider what we had to face.

Finances: The city was broke. Further, it had borrowed heavily and was dangerously in debt. And thus its credit ratings had dropped, which in turn made it more costly to sell its bonds.

The reason for its bankruptcy was a combination of outside forces—state and federal neglect—plus automatic increases in the cost of doing city business with a fixed tax base, plus the mounting costs of the urban poor. New York, like most other big cities, has a built-in budget gap no matter what it does. This is because expenses inevitably rise 15 per cent for the same level of services each year—because of labor settlements, because of the higher costs of goods and services, because of laws mandating certain levels of service. Revenues from city sources, however—real property taxes, licenses, etc.—increase only about 6 per cent annually. The state had traditionally reserved to itself more elastic forms of revenue, primarily the income tax.

Thus any city administration faced impossible choices. What had been done in the year before I took office was to borrow a quarter of a billion dollars to meet the operating expenses. This is still being paid off at a rate of $50 million a year, plus interest.

We also found a tax structure that had evidently been designed by a Rube Goldberg disciple on a bad trip. Substantive tax reform, reaching institutions such as banks, which had historically been treated with generosity, had apparently been deemed a political impossibility. Instead, a maze of taxes had been imposed on city-located businesses.

Each of those taxes was computed on a different base; they did not conform to state or federal practices; they added up to pure chaos for a businessman. Yet because real tax reform had not been undertaken for generations, it was the only way the city could imagine to raise revenues and avoid bankruptcy. And it wasn't working. Perhaps nothing symbolizes the state of our finances better than the discovery that the city reserves—money for emergency purposes—had dwindled from about $200 million to almost nothing in less than five years. We were draining a savings account to pay housekeeping costs. Clearly, sooner or later the money would be gone. These realities had never been faced head on.

The choice required was, then, no choice at all. We had to make basic changes in the structure of city finances. This meant that in my first year in office, as a member of a minority party in New York, I had to wage a long-drawn-out fight for basic tax reform, not in my own city, but in the state legislature, which controls (among other things) the New York City tax structures. I had to fight for a city income tax—not the most popular measure I have ever supported—and a commuter income tax, so that those millions of people who use the city but do not live here could be required to pay a portion of the costs for services they used. The legislators from suburban New York were remarkably unenthusiastic about this measure.

We did, in the summer of 1966, win our tax-reform program as well as substantial increases in state aid to New York. We ended the irrational tax that taxed gross business receipts instead of net income. We brought previously exempt institutions, like banks, into the revenue-gathering business. And we began a program of balancing budgets without borrowing, which we have maintained for four years.

The City's Economy: New York City's own fiscal structure was in bad shape. But just as alarming—perhaps more so—was the erosion of the economy within New York. By its very existence, New York is the center of corporate and business life in the United States; more than a third of the top five hundred corporations are here. Office-building construction has been on a steady upswing for years and neither the constant building nor the constantly higher rates can repress the demand.

Yet at the same time New York had a troubled economy. Along with other areas in the industrialized Northeast, New York was not holding its manufacturing base or its residential middle class. After World War II New York City lost 800,000 middle-class residents to the greener pastures of suburbia. In the same period about 10,000 manufacturing jobs were leaving New York City each year. Skilled labor was being drawn out of the city, which in turn encouraged businesses to locate elsewhere.

So this exodus would have been a problem regardless of the government. What was far worse was that it was treated as inevitable. It was not as though a bad policy was being used to fight the loss of economic strength in New York—there was *no* policy. There was not even a full-time Commissioner of Economic Development. There was no single center where a businessman could go for advice on zoning laws, city assistance, the hiring of skilled or unskilled labor, or small-business loans. The state and federal governments had correspondingly indifferent attitudes.

One of the tragic ironies in the midst of the decline was the existence of thousands of acres of land lying unused while industries moved out for lack of decent locations. The closing of the Brooklyn Navy Yard, for example, shut down a three-hundred-acre site ideally suited for many industries. The closing had been a real possibility for years, but no work at all had been done to find effective alternatives for use of the area. Similar if less famous tracts of land existed all around the city—tracts that were suited to industrial use and that could be developed in conjunction with job training for the semiskilled and with recreational and park land for residential communities nearby.

After a few years we saw the difference that could be made with a vigorous, full-time program of economic development. One-stop business aid was started to help a business concern cut through red tape in getting information and assistance. Industrial parks were completed at three places within the city, providing alternatives to dense, congested areas and freeing sites within nonindustrial sites for housing and recreation. Further, the whole basic idea of *planning* a site meant that we could include recreational and housing needs within an area even as we attracted business. The Brooklyn Navy Yard, after difficult wrangling, was finally transferred to the city to use, and within a few months concerns were already on site and job training for the unemployed was under way. Eventually as many as 40,000 jobs may spring from that one enterprise, not to mention the "multiplier" effect around the surrounding neighborhoods.

Basic Managerial Policy: In New York's Central Park, one of the great works of urban man, designer Frederick Olmstead built a walking path called The Ramble. Its charm lies in the fact that because of its meandering topography it is a place designed to get lost in—for courting, for thinking, for just being alone.

That is a good kind of planning for the park. Unfortunately, it seems to have inspired some of the men who had been running the government. For thirty years a ramble had been built up wherein it was almost impossible *not* to get lost—and for an administration trying desperately to help the city find itself, the outing was hardly pleasant.

We've heard often—indeed, I hear whenever I meet with a group of New Yorkers—horror stories about trying to get an answer from a bureaucracy. An ordinary citizen calling a department for a specific piece of information often finds it is the beginning of a long, long journey into anger and absurdity. Yet what is often not realized is that for those within the government itself the process of simply finding out what is happening can be equally frustrating. We found that this was all too true in the city. Thirty years of simply doing things because they had been done that way before made hard information almost impossible to get—and when we did get information, the picture was so grim that it might have been more reassuring never to have found out.

Take, for example, capital construction—the simple, mechanical process of building new city facilities. We knew before we came into office that the process took far too long. Yet when we took over and tried to begin locating the specific bottlenecks, we found that there was no description anywhere of the process of moving plans through to construction. It was just "done." And so no one could monitor the performance of construction. No one could really accelerate projects, because no one could look at a specific, step-by-step procedure. My new Commissioner of Public Works finally figured out that there were forty-nine separate steps in putting up a public building. Only then were we able to eliminate clearly overlapping steps, institute faster time schedules for each step, spot quickly where delays were occurring, speed up those projects (such as emergency hospital construction) that were critical, and draft legislation to eliminate many of the delays that were actually built into our laws.

This kind of vagueness was true no matter where we looked. Within the Police Department there was no central control for crime reporting, and local political pressures often affected the reported crime rate. (When we instituted a centrally controlled reporting system in my first year, reported crimes jumped 70 per cent—and almost 90 per cent of that jump was due solely to the improved reporting system.) The Police Department itself, badly in need of a new headquarters, had gotten a proposal in 1948. Seventeen years later the site-selection process still had not been completed. Meanwhile, the Sanitation Department was using obsolete trucks whose design was unlike those of every major city, adding to our expense because special trucks had to be designed for our use and special parts had to be ordered for repairing our trucks. Further, Sanitation had *no* preventive-maintenance program—the trucks, more than ten years old on the average, were simply driven until they broke down. Thus $9 million was spent every year on repairs, but nothing on preventing costly breakdowns—with the result that on any given day 40 per cent of our trucks were not operable.

Stories of conflicts, overlapping jurisdictions, and areas in which no department knew who had jurisdiction were legendary. For example, a complaint about water could be handled by the Buildings Department, the Health Department, or the Department of Water Supply, depending on whether the caller was complaining about no water, insufficient water, or insufficient *hot* water. Roads could come under the bailiwick of Highways, Parks, or the Triborough Bridge and Tunnel Authority; indeed, in one case, three different departments were responsible for an eight-mile stretch of road in Queens.

In the field of labor relations there was no policy; labor relations were handled by the Budget Bureau on an ad hoc basis and there was no overall record of the more than two hundred separate contracts between the city and its public employees. Only with the establishment of our Office of Collective Bargaining did a systematic program begin to emerge.

These were not isolated examples—they were in fact a reflection of thirty years of simple indifference to the ad hoc, unplanned growth of municipal bureaucracy. A civil-service force of 300,000 was itself trapped in this maze—and its very impotence in the face of an outmoded structure bred a severe crisis of confidence among New York's people. As the Task Force on City Personnel reported early in 1966: "The public has a poor impression of the city civil service, which has a damaging effect on city employees' morale and ultimately, therefore, on productivity." In other words, faced by anger on the other end of the phone and unable to perform simple duties, the civil servant was likely to conclude that frustration was inevitable and to resign himself to avoiding creativity and effort since it was obviously not rewarded within the structure of government.

What were the dimensions of this problem? Put bluntly, they were enormous. The city government had last been consolidated in 1938, and since that time twenty-nine new agencies had been established, with responsibilities ranging from civil defense and veterans' affairs to community mental health, from taxation to relocation. Each of them reported directly to the Mayor, as did a number of the hundred-odd different agencies, departments, and ad hoc commissions. Moreover, the only efforts at coordination were a welter of committees—nearly two hundred at one point—that were explicitly created to give the form, but not the substance, of coordination. And when we tried to find out what basic programs and policies were in effect, we often had to look for the work of committees that hadn't met in months. It was a normal occurrence to watch two different agencies pursuing contradictory plans for the same neighborhood because they had never bothered to talk to each other.

In spite of the 1961 charter reform, a strong Mayor still could not get things done if dozens of commissioners with overlapping jurisdictions and separate policies of their own were each responsible directly to the Mayor. There could be no effective delivery of services, no matter how strong the form, if the substance was not there—if city departments lacked the money to deliver services and the basic organizational knowledge to spot problems and respond to them. A charter mandate was important —but it could not work if the process of budgeting gave the Mayor no sense of overall policy, with each decision being taken without examining all the other decisions that would be affected. That, basically, was what had happened. The lift of government—the structure of government, the capacity to find out where things were going wrong—was not equal to the weight of its problems. And thus New York was trying to resolve jet-age problems with a jerry-built government. And it wasn't working.

It is not enough simply to look back at the delays and frustrations within the city government. The consequences of this kind of organization were felt in every neighborhood in New York by everyone who depended on the city for basic service and basic needs. It was here, perhaps, that the most dramatic evidence could be found to make the case that ours was a city in crisis.

One in four of our schools was more than forty years old—and an enormous Board of Education bureaucracy, attempting to run nine hundred schools from a central system, could not respond to the many complaints of peeling plaster, broken windows, and an absence of such necessities as books, paper, and chalk.

Our hospitals were in a state of disgrace, and worsening. In 1957 a health official said bitterly, "A man can't even die in dignity in Bellevue hospital." In 1965 conditions were worse. Of 8,000 nurses in the twenty-one municipal hospitals only 3,400 were registered nurses—the rest were aides who were barred from administering medication, thus adding to the registered nurses' burdens. At night it was common for a nurse to be responsible for fifty or more patients. I have seen hospitals whose windows had not been washed in a year, with roaches and filth everywhere, with unwashed sheets and unsterilized equipment. In one day members of my staff found more than a hundred violations at one hospital.

The whole area of planning for the future of the city was chaotic. Plans were being made for elevated expressways across two points in Manhattan that would have caused great dislocation and permanent harm to the communities affected, but no central planning group had the authority to raise basic questions about the environment. New housing was delayed as much as nine years while tenants were moved out of the area and forced to find inadequate housing that lacked even the solace of the familiarity of the old neighborhood. And although 250,000 units of publicly aided housing had been built since 1935, deteriorated housing was still a major problem. More than 700,000 units need replacement, basic rehabilitation, or upgrading. Pollution, unchecked by any effective municipal ordinance or policy, was so rampant that some ecologists questioned whether we could even breathe the city's air by the end of the century if prevailing trends continued.

What all this meant, of course, was that we found a breakdown in virtually every department of city government—a breakdown in structure and in coordination—and what that meant was a breakdown in something very important: the confidence of the citizenry.

Citizenry and the Government: At almost every turn, we were struck by the hostility between the citizens of New York and their government. In part, of course, this was a reflection of a general condition, a growing disenchantment at every level with the ability of government to meet the needs of the people. But there were other, more dangerous conditions in New York City—conditions that threatened to explode.

There was, for example, a growing sense of hostility between the police and residents in ghetto neighborhoods. This was as much a matter of suspicion as reality—police looked on ghetto residents, in some instances, as people who were indifferent to their attempts at strict law enforcement and who would not cooperate in apprehending criminals. To those in the ghetto, the deeds and acts of some policemen stained the whole department—brutality was alleged to be a common practice, as was corruption. Ironically, the police and the ghetto residents were often making the same mistake—attributing to everyone with a dark skin, or everyone who wore a uniform, traits they had witnessed only occasionally in one or two individuals.

But reality was not the problem. The problem was that the suspicions and hostilities of each group matched and reinforced the suspicions of the other. A suspicious policeman would utter an intemperate remark; the image of the policeman as a racist would be reinforced in the mind of the listener and would in turn condition *his* response to the next policeman he saw. And so it would go, without any attempt to open up lines of communication between policemen, who were there to protect a neighborhood, and that neighborhood, which desperately wanted better police protection.

To cite one extreme and explosive example, the year before I was elected Mayor the shooting of a black youth by a policeman had precipitated the worst riot in New York in decades, a riot that caused untold property damage and needless deaths and injuries on both sides. By early 1966, after Watts and with restlessness about ghetto conditions increasing rapidly, New York City was a powder keg—and on January 1 it became *our* powder keg.

For all the tension of police-community relations, however, perhaps a deeper problem lay in the general pessimism of the citizenry about the chances for improvement. They simply did not believe it was possible. Whether they were white middle-class homeowners or black ghetto dwellers, they had heard too much, been promised too much, seen too many pledges broken. You could not explain that a state law, or regulation 116-C, or failure to provide slip A-21 had set a project back six months, or a year, or three years. They saw—rightly—that a promise had not been kept. And with enough broken promises, with a continuing decline in city services and comfort, bitterness was replaced by resignation. "You can't fight City Hall" is shorthand for that feeling of impossibility about making the city better.

The worst part of all of this for me as a new Mayor was the realization that it would take years to make fundamental changes in the efficiency of the city government. Too much had been eaten away by neglect, too much had to be restructured. It was one thing to make myself visible, to meet more people, to bring more citizens' groups into the process of planning for New York. But it was quite another to begin delivering once the planning had been done. We were still burdened by the last thirty years of municipal organization, and no magic wand or brave speech could change it. I was, in effect, to be held culpable for a structure that I was actively, at time almost violently, seeking to change. I would be trying to govern a city with a procedure that I had condemned and that would be years in reshaping.

These, then, were some of the emoluments of office that I had not counted on. I do not believe there is anything more shocking to one who has just waged a campaign for office than to find out that things were even worse than he said they were. But that is precisely the state in which we found ourselves when we came into office. We *had* made campaign promises without a proper knowledge of what we would find, once elected.

There were, of course, all the other problems: a housing shortage that had grown by 100,000 units in the last five years, accompanied by a history of urban renewal that destroyed far more than it had ever built; a welfare system with no possibility of escape, and no programs to train those now receiving checks instead of a chance; traffic that had become the plague of our streets combined with an independent road-building authority committed to paving over green space and routing even more traffic into and through the core city; and an initial two weeks as Mayor spent in the throes of a transit strike.

But once the subways and buses were rolling, we found ourselves face to face with an overwhelming challenge: to govern a city that was going broke, that was in desperate need of new resources, that was very close to an explosion of violence, and that had lost the confidence of its citizenry. To use the strong language of a newspaper headline, we had to govern New York—"The City That Quit." We had to make it start working again.

V

Through the City Streets

WE REALIZED when we came into office that the city government was in urgent need of basic structural reorganization. But this takes time. You may plant new roots, or redesign ways of producing buildings, but the citizenry won't be convinced that City Hall has changed, that it is becoming more responsive to legitimate demands of citizens for a better voice in government and for better municipal services, unless something more immediate, more dramatic, occurs. Roots take time to grow; buildings take years to build. For people to regain hope, something visible is needed, now.

In 1966 this was particularly critical in our ghetto areas. I am well aware that in recent years I have been accused of "caring only about the blacks." Indeed, after only nine months in office I was greeted during a visit to a white neighborhood with the cry, "What are you doing here, Lindsay? White people live here."

It is true, I think, that in recognizing the demands of deprived neighborhoods for a sign of concern, we did not realize how much the vast bulk of city people—hard-working white middle-class citizens—felt estranged, too, from the process of government. We did, I know, recognize that in many critical areas of city life—safety, sanitation, transportation—the structure was not performing well for any of our citizens. But what we saw in early 1966 was that within the ghetto, discontent and alienation were at the breaking point. We saw that a basic commitment to ending that alienation through greater contact was essential. And we knew that words alone would not do the job. The people of the ghetto had heard all the words before. They had seen and heard the politicians who trooped into their neighborhood at election time, promising a new age. And they had seen them leave after the votes were counted, never to show concern by delivering reforms.

The consequences of this alienation were direct and explosive. There had been an explosion of violence in the summer of 1964 in Harlem. There had been greater explosions in Watts and dozens of other communities in 1965. And there was no question that the danger of more explosions was increasing as each month passed with no basic change in national policy, with each month that the needs of our cities—in job development and housing, health and education—were unfulfilled.

It is important to remember the fundamental daily impact of neglect in a poor neighborhood. For a middle-class community, separation from government means discontent and delays. For a person dependent on government for every essential need, an unresponsive bureaucracy can mean eviction from his home, loss of work, loss of food to feed his child. All the frustration that an ordinary citizen feels when he "fights City Hall" are multiplied by the stark fact that for an impoverished city dweller, indifference can literally be a matter of life and death.

It seemed to me critical, then, that the Mayor, having promised a basically new attitude in city government, demonstrate by a personal act of commitment that he meant what he said and that his concern would not cease after the election. In my 1965 campaign I had tried hard to break through the traditionally overwhelming Democratic vote in black neighborhoods, and I would often hear the call, "You'll forget us after November." I made a pledge to continue personal visits after the election. And the day after I won the mayoralty I revisited many of these neighborhoods, white and black, as a kind of symbol of the kind of concern I hoped to generate.

I found, instead, that mere visits were not enough, that people would not believe a symbol in the absence of an actual accomplishment, some continuing demonstration that the nonexistent links between citizen and community would be rebuilt. And thus the personal participation in the city came to be the start of the most urgent, basic effort the city government has ever made to structure contact between citizen and government. Many have read far too much into these visits to ghetto areas. They have been credited with single-handedly stopping riots, which is not true, and they have also been regarded as symbolically "buying off" black communities by promising to be permissive with law breakers and criminals, which is not true, either.

I think these visits did, however, offer some sign that the city government cared. They did suggest that this administration did not intend to exclude any group from the business of the city. And they did force all of us to listen to voices of angry discontent in every neighborhood. They did make us begin looking toward new ways of linking government and citizen. And to the extent that we began moving to break down the business-as-usual approach to running the city, I think that what we did was important and necessary.

Because so much national attention was focused on this activity, I think it is important to put a few facts into perspective. First, the overwhelming majority of these walks were unannounced, with the press excluded except for one representative from the newspapers. This was a matter of necessity. It has long been traditional to do sidewalk campaigning in the city, complete with camera crews and an enormous entourage. There was simply no benefit at all in producing another kind of road show; the chance for open contact between the people and myself would have been gone. We needed to do more than suggest concern—we had to deliver it.

Second, these visits were not the sole source of contact within neighborhoods, because I quickly discovered that without effective follow-up, the sense of involvement would vanish immediately. A person who complained personally to the Mayor about his garbage or police services might feel he had gotten something off his chest, but unless there was a permanent means of communication that feeling would quickly be replaced by further frustration and resignation.

I suppose the first direct involvement I had with a potential disturbance was in July 1966 during my first year in office, in East New York. East New York is a classic example of the urban melting pot. Located in east Brooklyn, it is a mixture—at times volatile—of Irish, German, Italian, and Polish citizens, with a more recent influx of blacks and Puerto Ricans. Almost simultaneously, two different disturbances broke out, one between blacks and Puerto Ricans, the other between whites and blacks in an informal "no-man's-land" between white and black neighborhoods. A small triangular-shaped park was the boundary; in this summer of 1966 that boundary had been crossed by the two groups of youths, each of whom was harassing the other.

In mid-July the trouble took the form of a small group of white youths who staged a picket line in this park. Calling themselves SPONGE—"Society for the Prevention of Negroes Getting Everything"—they marched and traded shouts with black youngsters for a period of about five days. The police responded by showing presence and by keeping the groups apart. But the Mayor's office was not immediately informed. Nobody—not the Youth Board, not the police—contacted the chief magistrate of New York City, the Mayor. This was not because of personal or professional oversight; it was simply that no system had ever been designed to give the Mayor's staff direct, speedy information about sources of possible trouble. And this in turn was because it was generally assumed that the Mayor had no responsibility in this matter. In the past, only when such trouble became a full-scale riot was the Mayor informed.

I first found out about the impending trouble after it had been brewing for a few nights and days. By that time the triangular park had become the focal point of fist fights, inflammatory remarks, and sparks of intense violence. I had toured nearby areas during my nightly walks earlier in the week, and it seemed quite natural that I go personally to the scene of disorder to get a clear sense of what had happened—and what might happen.

The basic memory I have of that visit was of unreality. We had no plan, no "theory" of what had to be done. We had only the knowledge that if we did not act, if we did not do all we could to preserve order, bloodshed and violence were inevitable. That night I visited East New York. You could feel the antagonism flowing across "no-man's-land." I walked through the white crowd to try and talk to the youths. I did not get a friendly reception.

"Go back to Africa, Lindsay, and take your niggers with you," I heard. After some tense moments we got ten of the youths into a bar on the "white" side of the dividing line and talked for an hour and a half. The conversation was blunt. "We don't want niggers in our neighborhood," they said. While this meeting was going on, I was informed that a group in the second trouble area in East New York—where black-Puerto Rican animosity was brewing—had been told the Mayor was coming. It was an uncertain moment, but I decided to stay where I was. A swift departure would only convince everyone that I was simply making an appearance. So I stayed and talked.

I got back to City Hall that night and was there barely an hour when word came that a youth had been shot and killed during sporadic shooting. The danger was obvious. Almost every racial conflict in every city has started with just such an event, where rumors fly ("A white cop shot a black boy") and mindless fury turns to violence. We knew that the police had done no shooting, that their command presence had been characterized by superb confidence and quiet force. But we did not know what the rumor mill was spreading. So we returned to the scene.

That was in some respects the longest night I have spent as Mayor. Along with assistants Barry Gottehrer, Jay Kriegel, and Sid Davidoff, I remained at the emergency Police Command post. Individual men were using all of their own lines into the community to talk, to dispel rumors. Human Rights Commissioner William Booth, Relocation Commissioner Frank Arricale, Mayoral Assistant Bob Blum, members of the Youth Board—all of them acted on their own, as they had to. There was no central contact.

The key, without doubt, was the work of the police. During the nights preceding the explosive spark and for three days afterward they were peace officers in the truest sense of the word. They were in a community that was at the breaking point. They were subjected to verbal abuse, taunts, assaults, and, at one point, gunfire. One wrong move and an all-out shooting conflict could have started. Instead, the police acted with a combination of massive presence and a refusal to employ lethal force unless directly attacked.

The first element was enough manpower to disperse any crowds and bring under control any potentially violent situation. At one point, seven hundred officers, fifty-four sergeants, forty-nine special foot posts, fourteen patrol-car posts, and dozens of detectives were on hand. They quickly dispersed knots of people and broke up conflicts. But the Police Command had determined that lethal force would not be used unless life was directly threatened. During the night, sniper fire was spotted from buildings, but the police waited until daybreak and in the morning cleared the buildings without firing a shot.

The police did instruct officers specifically to prevent looting and disorder by swiftly and efficiently arresting offenders and by removing them quickly from the scene before potentially dangerous crowds could gather. Helmets were issued to the men to reduce the chances of injury from thrown objects. Large numbers of men were employed to prevent officers from being outnumbered and overpowered. At the same time the Police Commissioner gave orders to cut down on the kind of provocations that could trigger emotional, irrational responses: sirens were not used, and specific instructions were issued to refrain from abusive or incendiary language. By establishing temporary headquarters at which large numbers of men were stationed, reinforcements could be speedily supplied. The police used bullhorns and sound trucks to issue announcements and control the crowds. When crowd formations grew, units of the Tactical Patrol Force, a special unit of the department, immediately approached the scene with about eighty men; they lined up and dispersed the crowd through their presence, thus combining force and restraint. Because of their silence in the face of shouts and taunts, clashes did not occur.

After a few days East New York calmed down. The careful planning by the police had been effective. But in the Mayor's office we were faced with a serious challenge. *Our* planning this first summer had been almost nonexistent. We had had no clear strategy—just instincts that had proved, in this instance, to be right. We had no permanent lines of communication, no continuing contact with the conflicting groups, no assurance that next week or next month a similar explosive situation would not occur. Indeed, by Friday night, in spite of the absence of widespread conflict, we realized that the weekend would bring with it unbearable tensions unless something was done. Thus, on the spur of the moment, we invited representatives from black and white groups to City Hall for a Saturday-morning meeting.

I do not think City Hall has ever witnessed that kind of meeting—the language and the exchanges were brutal. But it represented for these youths the first sign of any kind of communication with each other. At the end of the meeting we had somehow worked out an agreement for a joint effort to keep the area from exploding. Five people were designated as representatives to spread the word not to turn to violence. The whole arrangement, which was to begin that Saturday night, was jeopardized when we learned that a key member of the five had promised to take his wife for a drive and dinner that night. It took a mayoral phone call to persuade the wife to give up the evening. That man was on the streets of East New York Saturday night—and the neighborhood did calm down.

That was a combination of work and sweat and luck. But we could not let that kind of ad hoc operation continue as a strategy, because it was no strategy. All we knew at that point was that we knew little. The Police Department did have a strategy—but it was by necessity a strategy of response. The police could not be expected to do more than examine contingency plans for trouble. It was our job to see that trouble did not start. The roots of discontent did not lie in the conduct of police as much as it did in more basic conditions—the feeling that rationally going through channels led only into blind alleys. We had to provide something better than that—or else we would bear the consequences.

What we learned from East New York is that we had little real contact with communities. Early in my administration I had asked Barry Gottehrer and Sid Davidoff to serve as troubleshooters to give me and the city a direct link with local communities. What they discovered was that communication did not exist—that we were reacting to events instead of anticipating them, and that it was only *after* trouble broke out that we became aware of what we did not know. We saw, too, more basic flaws: that the city agencies themselves often had little contact with each other or with the diverse neighborhood voices that could really make a difference between a constructive community and one that was either indifferent or explosive. Indeed, city officials working in the same area often had little knowledge of each other's work, which made both communication and response to a specific neighborhood need very difficult.

Thus, throughout the fall of 1966 and into the spring of 1967 we made plans for a structured, formal link between neighborhoods and the city. In April of 1967 we announced, by mayoral executive order, the formation of the Summer Task Force, which would operate in nearly twenty neighborhoods throughout New York. Each local task force was headed by a high-ranking city official, to prove that we meant what we said about access to city government. We used a wide range of people—police officers, sanitation supervisors, assistants to the Mayor, commissioners and their deputies—to circumvent the slow channels of city response. In tapping community leaders we were without guidelines in uncharted waters. Davidoff, for example, found that athletes often were respected in the community, and in some neighborhoods persons without any "established" credentials of success could communicate with residents far better than conventional leaders. We did not hesitate to employ these people, because it was essential to make contact.

The Summer Task Force met at 8:00 A.M. each Monday morning during the summer of 1967. Because it had representatives from virtually every city department, it provided a ready forum for specific neighborhood complaints, ranging from police to sanitation to parks to housing. In many cases, heads of agencies recognized for the first time the extent to which their programs overlapped and competed with others and understood how coordination could improve their programs. We found, too, that detailed information was coming to the city administration that would enable us to spot sources of potential trouble. We learned which individuals, which groups, which gangs were in conflict on which streets of the city. We found out specifically which kinds of summer programs would be dismissed and which kinds could actually enlist the support of neighborhood youth. And we learned, most of all, how to talk to communities that had never been reached by any city voice except that of the bureaucracy or a law enforcer.

During the 1967 summer Barry Gottehrer, as the coordinator of the task force, received all reports of trouble—about a thousand of them. In two hundred cases that looked especially serious, Gottehrer got in touch directly with local task force leaders, who lived in the neighborhoods, who knew the people there, and who in fact acted as representatives from their neighborhoods to the city—instead of a representative of the city working in a neighborhood about which he knew little. On twenty-four occasions the task force leaders and Gottehrer took immediate action to head off an explosion.

This action took varied forms, depending on what was actually happening in the neighborhood. Sometimes, if the case involved a direct act by the city, I would go into the area, talk to the people, and attempt to make sure that a grievance was fully investigated. In East Harlem, after a policeman (black) shot a youth (Puerto Rican), the task force worked with the local parish to arrange a series of religious processions in the streets. Confrontation did not go away, but violence did not erupt.

In the Bronx protests against dirty streets became troublesome when residents began setting fire to garbage in the street. The police precinct commander and the task force leader immediately brought a sanitation truck to the area to remove the garbage, which eased tempers. In East New York the task force leader acted at the first eruption of violence to arrange a truce between whites and blacks—an act that succeeded only because he had won the trust of both groups in his work as task force leader. When a group of parents protested delay in the opening of a new school, the police summoned the task force and meetings were established with the Board of Education to talk about the matter.

In each case police could have arrested the dissidents—peacefully or forcefully. But the police, who are far more sophisticated than many of their self-styled "supporters," recognized that these acts were not crimes and that a mechanism existed that might restore order more quickly and at much less cost.

My own presence was confined to situations where police and task force members were convinced that it was necessary. There were times when my appearance would, in the judgment of the people on the scene, only have inflamed the situation. The Police Commissioner was always blunt in telling me his judgment, and I always accepted it. When I did go, it was frequently in a situation where wild rumors were spreading and where only the Mayor's voice could offer some counterweight to that kind of wildfire.

Of all the hot nights that I have spent in tense New York streets, the night that holds the most vivid memories for me was the night Martin Luther King was shot in Memphis, Tennessee—April 4, 1968. The shock waves were felt nationwide; in their wake, dozens of American cities exploded.

Mary and I began the evening at the theater, watching a new play in which a friend of ours, Tom Bosley, was playing the lead. The curtain was just rising for the second act when Detective Ernest Latty, New York Police, came down the aisle and called me from my seat to tell me the news. I went across the street and called Police Commissioner Howard Leary and Barry Gottehrer. They both reported that crowds were gathering on the streets of Harlem, Bedford-Stuyvesant in Brooklyn, and in part of the South Bronx.

I went back into the theater, told my wife the story, and headed for Gracie Mansion with Detective Latty. There I found Dave Garth, a friend and consultant on television and radio. A check with police revealed that matters were worse, and I headed for Harlem in our family station wagon. At 125th Street and Second Avenue I ordered the car stopped, asked Dave Garth to stay in it, and got out with Detective Latty and began walking westward on 125th Street. It was a route I had followed many times. But tonight it was different.

The crowds got thicker as we walked. It was a dark night, hot for spring, and you could feel the anger. Detective Latty, a black man himself, was worried. His job was to keep me from harm, and I knew he did not think I should be there—but he had felt that way on many other nights, and he knew he could not talk me out of it.

I put my hand on the shoulder of each man we passed, and expressed shared sorrow. There were no words spoken in exchange, only a nod of recognition. As we neared Lenox Avenue, we could feel the jostling and shoving—aimed not at me, but in the general way crowds move. At Lenox, we came to a police barricade across 125th Street, and there was a great deal of anger about it. "This is our street," one man said. "Why do they stop us from using it?"

I kept moving, but finally I was hemmed in from all sides. Occasionally I could hear my name shouted, and at other times I could hear men and women weeping or moaning. I was aware once in a while of groups of young men and boys running through the crowds down the street—and I heard sporadic sounds of breaking glass. Finally, I looked up and saw several very large black men on either side of me, all of whom I knew and had worked with. We edged to a clearing in the crowd, when another group of men moved close—also men I knew. The two groups began arguing about which was the better route for me to take. (It was later reported that I had been wedged in between hostile groups and had been driven off the street. In fact, the opposite was true. I was in the best of hands.)

Both groups were trying to stay by my side and keep me from any possible harm. I was finally steered over to a car driven by Percy Sutton, Borough President of Manhattan and a resident of Harlem. We drove back to Gracie Mansion, where I headed for the phones to check the city. It was tense in all of New York's black neighborhoods in four boroughs, with Harlem the most tense—but it was holding together. There were reports of looting in Harlem and Brooklyn.

By this time more staff had arrived and the phones to the task forces were in constant use. Reports from task forces all over the city were coming in—in other words, the concept was working. Someone pointed to the television sets in the office—we could see shots of flames in cities across the country. I located the Police Commissioner, who had arrived at 125th Street and had taken personal command of the police from a second-floor office on 125th Street. I mentioned to Commissioner Leary the antagonism toward the barricades. He said he had already seen that they were doing more harm than good and had ordered them removed.

By that time, having checked around New York again and having found Harlem still the most potentially dangerous area, I climbed back into the station wagon, which Dave Garth had by this time returned to the Mansion, and went back to Harlem. I joined Police Commissioner Leary in his makeshift second-floor office, and we watched developments—still tense, but still holding, with hundreds of helmeted police now on the street.

I finally left the building and again walked through the crowds, expressing sympathy as I walked, until I was at the end of the main crowds. The police were clearly in control by now and I returned to Gracie Mansion once again, to begin staff meetings and to make sure that the city was holding. It was and it did.

At the end of that first long, long summer, just when we thought we had gotten through the summer without a disastrous upheaval, a youth was shot and killed in Bedford-Stuyvesant. The rumor spread that a white policeman had shot an innocent, unarmed black child, and tension grew. One militant called up a mayoral assistant and said to him: "A white cop shot a black kid for no reason. This place is gonna burn. You tell that to your Mayor."

I went to the police precinct. I have never seen a crowd in an uglier mood. Youths were at the site of the shooting. The blood, which had not been cleaned up, was still spattered on the pavement. I met with about eight people in the captain's room at the precinct, and for a half hour listened to pure fury.

After the anger had subsided, I replied. Fortunately, I think, I was angry myself and showed it. I said something like: "Look. You've got two choices. You can burn down the community or you can change it. Now, do you want to burn it down? Is that what you want to do?" I think it was lucky that I did snap and reply with anger. They recognized that I was listening—that I was not reading from a script or telling them what I thought they wanted to hear. The very people who had made the loudest threats were subsequently instrumental in stopping rumors and helping to keep the peace. The same militant who had assured my assistant that "this place is gonna burn" later turned up as a spokesman against violence at that time. He did it not for me, but for himself.

It may seem as though the Summer Task Force was nothing but a peace-keeping operation, and indeed that was one of the original goals behind its establishment. The prevention of bloodshed and destruction should be a major city priority. But in fact the task force did more than that. Because of the diversity and the rank of those who served on it, it became a vehicle for community reconciliation and for spotting basic flaws in city services and correcting them. Almost by accident, the kind of policy coordination that every government talks about became a reality. Community and city spokesmen met regularly, so that vague promises that were not fulfilled could be swiftly challenged. Members of different agencies met together with local task forces, so that no official could slough off responsibility on another who might be in the same meeting. Representatives from the Mayor's office with direct access to me were at meetings, so that interagency conflicts could be resolved then and there, in many cases.

Eventually, participation in the task force included elected officials or their aides—city councilmen, state assemblymen and senators, and national congressmen joined in the meetings. Private groups were brought in; civic groups, churches, schools, veteran and business organizations all recognized that the task force was a new kind of mechanism, supported by direct mayoral commitment and able to act, in many instances, with speed and effectiveness.

The task force, for example, succeeded in raising funds from private sources to put recreational programs into areas that lacked parks, playgrounds, and other places for children to play during the summer months. Basketball, softball, and volleyball leagues were begun in Far Rockaway. Children were taken by bus out of the city for a day, Arts-and-crafts programs were begun in neighborhoods where young residents had never worked with any creative tools.

One of the key elements, in keeping with the task force principle, was to hire neighborhood youths as supervisors. In one sense this was a risk, as many of these youths had been in trouble, dropped out of school, or run afoul of the law. But, as one recreational supervisor noted, "We hired indigenous kids and got them to organize teams. You know, all these kids want is a little responsibility and a feeling someone really respects them."

The truth of this observation was demonstrated by the task force programs. Of course, there were dropouts and mistakes and there was conflict. Had we wanted a trouble-free program we would have had no program. But the clear pattern that emerged was that with responsibility and with programs, both those who supervised and those who participated created a vibrant, important new asset for the city—and they did it largely by themselves.

More basically, the task force enabled representatives from communities to meet with city officials about basic services. This kind of contact of necessity went beyond peace-keeping to basic weaknesses in the city structure. Residents complained about garbage pickups that did not meet schedules. They complained of abandoned housing not yet torn down and of capital-construction projects of schools and hospitals that had been long delayed. And here the problem became clear: it was relatively easy to supply programs for the summer. Broadway in the Streets, Jazzmobiles, street-theater programs, recreational activity —all of these could be supplied through the generosity of private contributors and hard work by city and neighborhood people. But with the more basic complaints—"Why doesn't the school teach our children?" "Why don't we have more police?" "Why isn't there low-income housing here?"—the discussions got into basic structural weaknesses of the city government and the insufficient response of the state and federal governments. A city that lacks money cannot answer these complaints, no matter how responsive it wants to be. It cannot cut services to one neighborhood or cut back on police to provide more sanitationmen. All it can do is explain.

But, as I have already noted, explanations do not remove grievances. A community that has learned to organize and seen responses to some problems will not rest content with the statement that the city lacks money. They want results. And they, like every other group in the city, are entitled to them. So, in a sense, the task force helped to focus discontents and to increase dissatisfactions. It was, in that sense, the kind of result that would seem, politically, to have been a mistake.

But it was not. For it brought the ghetto areas of the city into steady, regular contact with the city for the first time. It offered something besides the faceless, soothing city official who offered nothing but delays or inaction. It forced city officials to face up to basic weaknesses in their departments and in the city as a whole. And it delivered on promises.

Perhaps the best judgment on the task force was summed up in a telegram to me from a Brooklyn task force after the summer of 1967. It urged the creation of a year-round task force, stating correctly that "the problems of the ghetto cannot be alleviated by temporary cooling programs during the hot summer months. If the concern of the city administration is not demonstrated on a year-round basis, it is doubtful whether community support can continue to be mustered for emergency situations."

Thus, in September 1967, the city created the Urban Action Task Force on a year-round basis. And a few months later the task forces began to work in middle-income communities as well as in the ghettos. These communities—with serious problems of their own—had seen in ghetto neighborhoods a new source of community organization and direct access to the city, and they began to complain that city resources were being diverted from their neighborhoods to those in which the task forces were operating. It was a false assumption, but it did indicate the extent to which the task forces—direct contact between neighborhoods and the city—had achieved success. They had in fact alerted the city and its people to a workable alternative to red tape.

At present, task forces are at work in forty-four neighborhoods of every kind in New York, attempting to answer specific community needs, whatever they may be. And here again is a demonstration that in the last analysis the city requires basic changes to answer demands for better services.

It can be said, then, that this whole program grew out of an initial decision to become a visible, accessible mayor whose administration was at work in the neighborhoods of New York. It would be nice to say that this was a carefully planned, "gamed-out" strategy, applied calmly and surely at every stage. It would be nice to say that—but it wasn't the case. In fact, it grew bit by bit and piece by piece: each finding required a new form of response, and each success in establishing contact between city and community required an extension of the idea.

The task force, however, did not end my own decision to continue walking the streets. There are many reasons for this. In the first place, I think nothing is more dangerous to an executive than isolation from the people and reliance on advisers who, however competent, may tend to tell the executive what they think he wants to hear. It's not very likely that an aide will say, "Mr. Mayor, they think you're a nigger lover in my neighborhood and they hate you for it." But it is likely that in some neighborhoods that is precisely what I will hear.

Second, and more important, I think it necessary to get as much of the flavor of the city as possible. New York is a city of dozens of neighborhoods, each one different, each one unique. There are moments of priceless contact—some of them humorous, some of them poignant—that no briefing sheet or news summary can give. That's why I have tried to make as many of these unannounced small walking tours as possible.

There was the time, early in my administration, when I was in Harlem and a tall black youth determinedly pursued me down the street saying, "Mr. Mayor, I want to talk to you." He looked troublesome and I ignored him until I had moved away from the larger crowds on the street. Then I turned and faced him. He said slowly, "Hey, Mr. Mayor, how come you wear a *green* tie with a *blue* suit?"

There are times when a young man will ask me, with calm urgency, for a job—any kind of job—so he can support his family in dignity. There are the personal-concern comments—"You look too thin—you look tired." There are expressions of good will and not-so-good will, the complaints about inadequate city services, the sights and sounds of neighborhoods that are thriving, or decayed, or a strange mixture of both.

And then there are the times when there is no satisfaction or hope or determination—only the kind of rage that makes me realize what lofty terms like "urban crisis" and "polarization" mean.

There was the visit to the home of a woman who had been killed in a senseless accident during a street conflict. It was a dark, small apartment crammed with children silent and dazed. The husband, now a widower because of an act of madness, sat silent. On the wall, from Fort Gordon, Georgia, was a plaque that read: "Peace and Plenty."

There was the visit to an angry mob, restless and volatile because of the shooting of a youth. It was a short, grim meeting. I spoke briefly, promised an investigation, and asked them to go home in peace. They did. And yet you wonder what can really be said to turn a violent reaction to a violent act into something that is not going to kindle more destruction. And you wonder how many incidents on how many nights it will take before no words can be spoken.

There was a brief discussion with a seventy-nine-year-old woman, one of a million people over sixty-five who live in the city on incomes far below the poverty level, many of them leading lives that are desperately lonely.

"My children say 'hang yourself,' " she says. "I didn't turn on the gas only because I didn't want to leave a big bill."

What about a nursing home, her welfare caseworker asks.

"I'll turn the gas on," she says. "I'll join my husband, such a handsome, happy man, why did they have to take him away from me?"

There is a young white boy, just out of jail.

Why were you in?

"I was on welfare," he says. "I hadn't gotten a check. I was stealing food and I had burglar tools."

Why? "I was hoping to get caught."

There was the visit to a stable, clean neighborhood, without the visible scars of poverty but with problems just as real. You talk to people whose parents came to New York as immigrants and whose own effort brought them out of poverty into a better life. They now face a world where their higher economic status is not really that much higher, because of inflation and taxes, where they cannot see how they will send their children to college or how they will pay for emergency medical expenses. And they see and hear a lot of talk about black and Puerto Rican needs, but not about their own.

Some of them equate black militancy with crime. Some believe that educational programs for ghetto children will jeopardize their own children's chances for college. Some believe that the city administration does not care about whites or about those who live outside of Manhattan.

You can't give the whole answer. You can't talk about efforts to improve the quality of life in their neighborhoods—about the new transit systems and schools and health centers that are still years away from completion—because they cannot be produced immediately and therefore seem unreal. You cannot talk about the attempt to answer the sharply disparate needs of a hundred communities or the fact that no child will be excluded from a city university who has met the standards of admission. All you can do is to try and talk about the work you have done. Sometimes they listen . . . sometimes they do not.

Yet I still believe that a Mayor must be visible—that he must be a part of the city he tries to lead. It is clear that walks and personal meetings are not substitutes for better services or more money or programs to meet the demands of the citizenry. But I also think that a man cannot be the Mayor of a city if he is unwilling to provide access to his administration, and to himself.

I do not believe any future Mayor of New York will be allowed to retreat into his office and deal with the city as a separate entity. There is no guarantee that visibility and communication will result in basic reforms. But without a personal demonstration of concern, I do not think a city administration can hope to lead effectively or govern well.

VI

Participation and Delivery

THE RESPONSE TO THE Urban Action Task Force and personal visits to city neighborhoods gave impressive evidence that the people of New York felt far removed from their government and that dramatic steps were necessary to begin breaking down the barriers that had been building up for so long. But clearly these steps were not enough. Task forces can report quickly the discontents and needs of different neighborhoods and visits by the Mayor can give symbolic evidence of concern, but they cannot, by themselves, overcome the increasing disaffection with which the people of our cities, and our society in general, hold the institutions of government. The symptoms and the causes of this disaffection run far, far deeper than vague dissatisfactions with unresponsive bureaucracies. They reach into the basic structure of government today.

Perhaps the strongest evidence of this feeling was the rhetoric of the 1968 presidential campaign. Almost without exception, the candidates for the nominations of both major parties attempted to touch this sense that government had grown too distant and too powerful. Ronald

Reagan called himself a "citizen-politician" without ties to bureaucracies; Richard Nixon said that the federal government had to return power to the state and local governments; Nelson Rockefeller mentioned "the new politics" of citizen participation. The Democrats, too, long the party of a strong federal government, began to speak of participation. Eugene McCarthy used his primary campaign as a demonstration of direct citizen involvement in governmental affairs. Robert Kennedy, one of the first to speak of this approach shortly after his election to the Senate, supported revenue sharing, decentralization, and community corporations. Even Hubert Humphrey, perhaps the symbol of old-time liberalism, urged the government to involve the citizenry more closely in decision making.

In some ways, the entire campaign of George Wallace was an attempt to spark the concept of a citizens' revolt against their government. In addition to the clear streak of racism that ran through his efforts, Wallace spoke of the "little man"—"the steelworker and the cab driver, the barber and the beautician"—as victims of an all-powerful establishment composed of "guideline writers" and "pseudo-intellectuals who can't park a bicycle straight but want to tell you what time to get up in the morning and what time to go to sleep at night." And he promised that if he became President he'd "take their briefcases and throw them in the Potomac River."

There is no question, then, that this sense of distance, this demand for a feeling of self-destiny, is becoming a dominant theme of contemporary politics, cutting across ideological lines, blurring the distinction between right and left, and forcing governments to respond in some way to this sense of loss.

It is most strong, perhaps, in city government, for this is the level that is supposed to be closest to the people, that is directly responsible for their basic well-being: the safety of their streets and homes, the condition of their neighborhoods, the protection against health hazards, the state of their hospitals and schools. Yet the fact is that in any large city, and most dramatically in a city of 8 million people, there is little that an individual citizen can do about the quality of these services, and it is partly for that reason that the quality has declined.

This self-destiny thesis is in conflict with the conventional political wisdom of city government. For years it was argued that the city was a giant conglomerate to be run as a centralized decision-making power with policies charted and decisions made by individuals who have the training and experience to administer programs properly. This concept gained powerful momentum during the drive for reform in the early decades of the century, when it was considered critical to "take the city out of politics." Centralization is even more necessary now, some claim, because long-range planning has become critical to the future of the metropolis. With hundreds of suburban governments surrounding our cities, with national decisions directly affecting the life of the city, with air and water pollution requiring regional compacts, only centralized planning can protect the safety of the metropolis and insure the delivery of services.

This is a perfectly reasonable theory. The only problem is that it is oversimplified and is not borne out by the facts.

Consider, first, what has happened to city government in New York. As I have already discussed, when we took office we found a governmental structure that had grown so large, so unwieldy, so enormous that it literally did not know what it was doing. It had become so disjointed that a complaint about a street was the province of the Highway Department, a complaint about a small bridge was the responsibility of no city agency, a complaint about a route through a park went to the Parks Department, and a problem with a major bridge was referred to the Triborough Bridge and Tunnel Authority. While the foregoing was true in many cases, there were as many others in which decisions were centralized and a multitude of complaints—in a city with the population of a small nation—had to go through one common department, making it a Herculean labor for an ordinary citizen to get a grievance redressed.

The schools were in a similar state. In all the controversy and turmoil that has surrounded the school system in recent years, one essential fact remained—a Board of Education composed of a few people had to make basic educational policy for more than a million children scattered through nine hundred schools. And an archaic staff structure had the responsibility for supplying basic educational services to the schools in the city.

This condition is general throughout most city governments in America. There is not a mayor in the country who could not produce a thousand letters, each detailing a horror story of what happened to one citizen seeking to get a simple complaint answered. The shuffling among departments and agencies, the lack of information, the absence of any center for decisional responsibility—all these are commonplace in city government, which moves many people to think it is based on an idea by Franz

Kafka.

No one disputes the need for sensible organization of the city government—it has certainly received top priority during my years as Mayor. One of the most important things my administration has done is to gain central control of decisions that were previously made with no control *at all.* The Policy Planning Council and the Program Planning Budgeting System (PPBS) that we established in the Budget Bureau give the city, for the first time, information about exactly where money can most effectively be used. We now know specifically what it costs to implement new programs and whether new alternatives will give us a better run for our scarce money. We know what services we can trade off for new programs and whether inefficient efforts can be salvaged or must be abandoned.

We have brought in outside management experts, such as the Rand Corporation, to help coordinate city government, to tell us, for example, whether a fundamental transportation decision has been based on correct or faulty assumptions (will a population shift perhaps render a new transit route irrelevant, and are we neglecting city growth elsewhere?). All of this is vital—and it achieves, in a sense, a centralization of perspective and judgment. But it does not make the case against community participation weaker. It tells us, instead, that in the past authority was centralized but capacity was lacking.

Just as surely, no one disputes the need for a concept of regional planning directed at preserving urban and undeveloped environments. All of us have seen the consequences of chaotic, uncontrolled land use: the growing spoilation of waters that has turned our own Hudson River into an open sewer; the corruption of the air by chemicals and pollutants that pose a direct threat to health and life; the disappearance of open land and livable urban neighborhoods to the bulldozer; the unregulated suburban sprawl that offers neither a natural setting nor a sense of community.

We require regional agreements and even national legislation in a variety of fields such as that provided by the Air Quality Act and Clean Air Act, both of which give financial assistance and set federal restrictions on pollutants in the air. Similarly, parkland and wilderness areas require broad legislative policies to preserve them from exploitation and destruction. Planning is necessary in the cities so that we do not build massive housing developments without protecting recreational land, preserving neighborhoods, and providing transportation and other municipal services for the people who live there.

The issue, then, is not whether we should plan but *how*: who is to be consulted, what decision mechanisms are to be used, how that delay which turns innovation into obsolescence is to be avoided. In essence, after four years as Mayor my belief is this: we cannot plan for the citizenry unless we plan with them, unless we are willing to give to individuals, to neighborhoods, and to communities the power to be heard and the power to challenge, the power most of all to actually decide as much as is possible what their communities will look like and how they will work.

I advise those who believe that such increased participation will produce fragmentation to look at the record. The history of the last fifty years is replete with examples of a single all-powerful decision-making body planning neither democratically nor comprehensively, and creating major dilemmas for the future.

There was, for example, nothing fragmented about the highway program, nor was any concept of consultation built into it. In New York highways were designed and built by the Triborough Bridge and Tunnel Authority, an independent body which has virtually no check on its power and which has plenary authority to plan and build roads for the flow of traffic in the metropolitan region.

But this concentration of authority did not prevent short-sightedness. It did not prevent the gutting of neighborhoods, the overcrowding of city streets with autos, or the construction of highways along the shores of Manhattan Island that have cut off its people from the city's waterfront and have severely limited the recreational possibilities of the city. It did not provide for effective and integrated planning for the city. In fact, because of the power of the highway planners and their single-minded concern with building roads, proposals for highways were almost guaranteed to be crippling to the greater interests of New York. At one time the highway interests proposed elevated expressways across both the center of Manhattan and lower Manhattan; the first would have displaced some 5,000 residents and 2,000 businesses and created instant slums in adjoining areas. In other words, the very act of vesting so much decision-making power in one body with a single, narrow interest has produced the antithesis of good planning and delivery of services.

Similarly, the initial public-housing policies, designed to replace slums with new housing, included no process for consultation with the residents of the affected neighborhoods; decisions were made solely between the city and Washington. Here again, the lack of participation directly interfered with the delivery of good, well-planned housing, for the planners had almost no contact with the people and their interests; these nonpolitical experts simply assumed that this kind of housing was desirable. The consequence was a spate of badly designed housing projects that either clashed with the surrounding neighborhood or helped to destroy it by demolishing important centers of community life—stores, streets, taverns, and that indefinable set of services which make a neighborhood pleasant. No one asked whether the residents would have preferred to rehabilitate bad housing in the context of the existing community, or whether the proposed housing was acceptable. It was built; people were relocated; and the city suffered.

Moreover, the centralization of authority was something less than a smashing success even in providing the housing scheduled by the urban-renewal program. Delays of a dozen years or more were common, and by 1969 the program in New York City had not even kept pace with deterioration. Indeed, under the urban-renewal programs of the early 1950's what often happened was that low- and moderate-income housing was torn down and relatively high-income housing was built—housing that the displaced residents could not afford.

Poor planning, then, is a danger when government and the citizenry lose touch with each other. But it is not the only drawback of this top-down method of decision making. We must understand that Americans, across all lines of race and background, class and age, have paid a high price for distant, impersonal power. That price is the pervasive, deepening sense that citizens and government are no longer pursuing common ends; that individuals can do nothing about the quality and direction of the neighborhoods they live in, nor even about their own lives; that faceless bureaucrats who neither understand nor care about what people want have the nation's destiny in their hands.

I do not believe we can continue to pay this price—in the ghettos, in the working-class and middle-class neighborhoods, in the suburban communities, in rural areas. And I do not believe the American people, wherever they live, are willing to pay it any longer.

I believe, rather, that those responsibile for government—local, state, and federal officials—must begin to open the way for participation and toward growing autonomy for citizens as citizens, in their own communities. Further, I believe that we will gain from this new kind of planning not simply more participation, but better planning, better delivery of services, and even the beginnings of a restored faith of the people in their government.

For the past three years we have attempted to move toward this goal in New York City. We are a long way from realizing it. We have made many mistakes and encountered a great many difficulties in breaking through the traditions of the past and the understandable inertia of the bureaucracy of municipal government. The city is still unresponsive to the demands of many groups in New York, and at times is unwilling to share enough decision-making power with them. And we continue to face outdated attitudes and unresponsiveness from state and federal systems. Nevertheless I think we have made important progress, and I think we have proven that, in spite of all the problems it can bring, participation is well worth the effort.

The first step is to establish a citizens' mechanism to overcome the frustration that all government breeds, that feeling that governments, at every level, are nothing more than endless mazes of departments and bureaus in which a complaint is either lost, ignored, or forgotten. We found early in our administration that frustration was obsessive in ghetto neighborhoods, where in many cases there simply was no means of communication with the city.

The creation of the Urban Action Task Force demonstrated that contact between communities and city agencies was possible. But the task force was not enough. We believed it imperative to have throughout the city local branches of the government to which citizens could bring any complaints relating to the performance of the city government. In my 1965 campaign, I pledged to establish "neighborhood city halls" to help citizens wind their way through the red tape when seeking assistance. This proposal drew substantial opposition, particularly from those involved in the then-prevailing political machinery. In addition to being suspicious of the political implications of neighborhood city halls, many feared that such centers would deprive political clubs of their function of providing help to voters—a function long considered important to the continued vitality of political organizations in big cities.

Consequently, the City Council refused to provide funds for neighborhood city halls, and we were forced to rely on private funding, which limited the number of such offices. Despite this setback, however, the results were almost immediately encouraging, especially in those areas where the neighborhood city hall became the nucleus of the Urban Action Task Force.

For example, more than 2,300 problems were brought to the city's attention through one neighborhood city hall located in a city-owned health center in Queens. The complaints ran the gamut from housing to street and sewer conditions, from abandoned cars to welfare problems and requests for traffic lights—all the services a city tries to provide for its people. The hall was staffed by three professionals supplemented by volunteers from the neighborhood who took it upon themselves to become actively involved in the community, both as residents and as "ombudsmen," informal citizen advocates who could channel complaints and problems directly into the machinery of the city administration.

The results were impressive. The number of cases handled jumped from 2,200 in 1967 to more than 8,000 in the first nine months of 1968. More important, however, was the fact that as local residents realized their neighborhood city hall was an effective mechanism for getting grievances resolved, they became willing and even eager to use it as a center for increased community participation in city planning.

One of their problems concerned derelicts who congregated near a stretch of liquor stores on a major thoroughfare. They were not hard-core criminals; they simply had no place else to go. The neighborhood city hall acquired a vacant lot for these men and turned it into a card-playing area, maintained and policed by those who used it. The hall also found a storefront the men could use in the wintertime. This was, of course, a small step, and did not begin to solve fundamental problems. But it was a step from which the community benefited and which it could take on its own, without having to go through the endless delay of centralized decision making.

Similarly, the hall was able to cut through one of those ill-considered planning decisions that often afflict city government. The Parks Department had decided to build a public swimming pool on a site along the direct flight pattern into LaGuardia Airport, a location considered dangerous by the people who lived there. The decision had been made without consulting either community groups or the neighborhood city hall. The neighborhood city hall, in a move that would have been unheard-of under previous administrations, actually helped organize the protests against the city department, and ultimately succeeded in locating the pool in a neighborhood that wanted it, and to which, in fact, it had originally been promised.

Once again, this action did not hail the millennium in New York City. It did not solve the major problem of inadequate resources nor did it prevent other delays. But it illustrates how the city can help itself by creating mechanisms to improve its performance, and can do so as a direct result of community involvement. Equally important, these mechanisms also served as vehicles for bringing groups together.

This procedure can be expanded into far broader uses. Many advocate the establishment of community corporations in poor neighborhoods to coordinate the flow of help from city, state, and federal agencies and to plan economic development, and there is no reason why neighborhood city halls cannot serve this purpose too, particularly in neighborhoods where poverty is not the main problem but where city services still need great improvement and where it is increasingly important for groups to talk with each other. It can be the center for community complaints, thereby providing an alternative both to fruitless treks through municipal corridors and the protests and confrontations born of a desperate attempt to attract the attention of somebody in authority. It can also be a center for community discussion when friction arises between groups.

It can serve as a forum for the local representatives of the City Planning Commission or of local planning boards. Proposals for major urban development can be unveiled there while still in the early stages, thus supplying the means of communicating between the city and the citizenry. Instead of recriminations after a proposal has been completely planned, authentic consultation between concerned groups is possible so that final development represents as much unanimity as possible. Of course, this does not end all disputes, since on some occasions interests might be irreconcilable. But it works, and the neighborhood city halls we have been able to open have proved it.

We learned this when we proposed a water-pollution-control plant to be built on the edge of the Hudson River on the Upper West Side. Residents of the neighborhood feared that the plant would replace recreational area and blight their community. The conventional solution would have been to weigh pollution control against recreation and argue that pollution was more important.

We tried something else. We invited representatives from the city, the local planning board, and other community groups to form a steering committee to negotiate alternatives. The result was a plant that included recreational facilities and aesthetic features in its design that would actually improve the neighborhood. This did more than virtually eliminate opposition—it also eliminated the long, dreary procession of lawsuits and political bickering, demonstrations and rallies which inevitably cause delays. It sped up the project as well as improved it, and put the citizens of the neighborhood in the position of authentically influencing the health of their community. This is the kind of process, institutionalized through neighborhood city halls, that could be one of the most powerful methods of reviving the sense of self-destiny which makes communities not only vital but willing to work with city government.

The concept of extending the voice of the community has been tried in a wide range of areas. We have, for example, experimented with expanded police precinct councils in an effort to break down the mutual misunderstandings between police and residents of ghetto neighborhoods which weakens both crime prevention and the confidence of the community in the process of law enforcement. The aims of the councils are simple: to emphasize the mutual interdependence of the police and the community in maintaining public safety, to develop mutual respect, and to promote an atmosphere conducive to greater public cooperation.

Briefly, the councils meet in police precincts to discuss an open-ended agenda ranging from police explanations of the importance of getting effective cooperation in law enforcement to citizens' allegations of inefficient or unjust police practices. It has not been an easy program to establish. Those most suspicious of the police and those with the least stake in society—the dropout, the jobless—do not participate frequently, while those who are well established in their neighborhoods do participate, but they are usually the least in need of help. Nevertheless, the councils have helped to break down the familiar, inaccurate stereotypes of the lawless ghetto dweller and the brutal policeman. Many participants have come to recognize the human being behind the clichés and to that extent the councils have served a useful purpose. Moreover, they have helped to build joint police-community efforts, both in crime control and in matters of broader community concern.

This kind of participation is, at least to begin with, another small step. While projects such as neighborhood city halls and police precinct councils can in fact undertake broad planning functions, they are essentially mechanisms to exchange information to provide the city with current, honest information on problems within communities.

That same kind of effort has been made in other areas, such as providing twenty-four-hour service in the Mayor's office. City government has ceased to be looked at as a nine-to-five operation, to be shut down in the evening and opened again the next morning. Citizens, I suppose, used to be expected to manage their lives so that crises did not occur in the intervening hours. We have found that the use of a "Night Mayor"—a city official on duty throughout the night—enables us to avoid disasters that could arise if an emergency went unattended.

Finally, we have tried to make wide use of volunteers for city service. Chiefly under the leadership of Deputy

Mayor Timothy Costello, we have established a number of internship programs in city government. Our Urban Corps involves more than 2,500 college and graduate students on a summer and part-time basis. With foundation support, we have started a year-round fellowship program for qualified students to take a paid "urban sabattical." More than 25,000 volunteers are part of our auxiliary police (for which the city provides uniforms and training), and more are joining newly formed "tenant patrols" to help combat crime in city housing. And every night, from 5:00 P.M. to 11:00 P.M., a team of citizen volunteers mans the phones in the basement of City Hall in the Mayor's "Action Center" to answer questions from New Yorkers about getting help from the city.

These reforms are, however, only the beginning. Far more difficult is the job of bringing the citizenry into long-term neighborhood development and providing a viable system of consultation. I want to emphasize again that our record in this field is not perfect. In some neighborhoods we have not followed through in our commitment to consult; in others, conflicts between the city and the community have simply been irreconcilable. But what we have done convinces me that participation can and must be increased, and that even in the most complex areas of urban development it can make possible a more efficient as well as a more democratic system of government.

One such step was prompted by the Community Action Program of the War on Poverty, which called for efforts to be directed and controlled with the "maximum feasible participation" of the groups to be served—i.e., the poor. This effort has been an enormously complex one and has produced reactions ranging from enthusiasm to cynicism to outright fear. In effect, the program reached out to communities that had never known any degree of economic power and offered them large amounts of both power and resources within a structure that provided independence from the established, organized political machinery.

This kind of program was bound to produce conflicts, and of course it did. Rival local groups competed for power, and because the competition was outside the structure of the established political parties, which can help to resolve competition, it was frequently less orderly, and thus more unsettling, than traditional political contests. Because of the elusiveness of the concept of "community," those in power were frequently accused by those who were not of mismanagement or betrayal.

And yet, for all the conflict, it did produce one undeniable conclusion: in spite of the frequently heard assertion that ghettos lack leadership, some of the most competent and aware individuals in the city at last discovered that they could make a difference. After discounting all the disputes, it became clear that the potential for self-help and self-reliance was present in the poorest, most deprived neighborhoods of New York City to an extent undreamed of by past leaders. School dropouts, welfare mothers, one-time hustlers, all provided articulate and effective spokesmen for their concerns.

Whatever reforms must be made in the effort to fight poverty—and I believe there are substantial redirections that are essential—I think it is clear that we can never go back again to the system of top-down direction. These communities want the chance to plan their own improvement and to engage their own men and women in the job of rebuilding themselves. They are still distrustful of the city government; still cynical about the *totally* unseen state and federal governments; still dubious that commitment will be supported by adequate resources. But they have demonstrated both their willingness to work for peaceful change and their capacity to bear more than their share of the load. In my judgment, that capacity and that willingness must be nurtured and supported, not just because it is realistic, but because it is in the best tradition of self-reliance, a commodity that has been tapped far too infrequently by governments. It is right to offer our citizens the power to govern themselves—and it is also necessary.

A newer, far more exciting and thoroughgoing example of participation lies in the Model Cities Program. Funded by federal and city resources, this program is rooted in the principle that no effort in any field will be successful unless it is part of a general effort to improve conditions. Specifically, you shouldn't design housing unless you also plan for transportation and crime prevention and recreational space; you shouldn't design community health facilities without tying them to day-care facilities, Head Start programs, and other social-action projects.

Thus, planning for development across the board in a community is an integral part of the Model Cities efforts. Members of the basic committee are chosen from the neighborhoods through the ballot—and built-in mechanisms are intended to insure maximum consultation with the people affected. This body, in turn, is given a large measure of authority to design the services for its neighborhood.

The city, of course, must be willing to cooperate with these bodies—and this is not always easy. At times there are strong antagonisms between those in the traditional service departments—such as sanitation and housing—and those community spokesmen who are neither satisfied with the level of services nor sympathetic to the strictures of existing departmental procedures. In addition, a long history of uncoordinated efforts among city departments has made it difficult to achieve cooperation in Model Cities efforts.

Nonetheless, there is reason for hope. We have found that once people understand that they are really part of the decision-making process, their attitudes change rapidly. They become less concerned with futile protest or confrontation because, since they possess the power to *do* something about their complaints, they are far more likely to channel their discontent into efforts to create alternatives.

The results are sometimes startling, as they were in a case in Brooklyn where a housing development in Coney Island had been stalled for nine years because of continuing disputes between the city and community groups. We decided to try the Model Cities approach there, even though some people felt that opening up the decision-making process to a new group of spokesmen would only cause further delay. But the Housing and Development Administration met with two local groups and worked out a compromise plan which, although it completely satisfied no one, all agreed to live with.

Less than a year after the Model Cities effort was begun, the obstacles to the development were overcome and construction was ready to begin. Similarly, we have found a significant easing of mistrust between neighborhoods and city agencies through the dispersion of power. After they were given authentic authority, neighborhood groups recognized that their role was in fact a positive one: to help develop and preserve their neighborhoods instead of simply protesting decisions over which they had no real control.

We have tried, too, to incorporate these lessons into general rules for city policy. For example, in our housing program we have moved as far as possible from the emphasis on high-rise monstrosities that shut out sunlight, produce sterile neighborhoods, and satisfy no one. Instead, we have moved toward "vest-pocket" housing, building in smaller, totally deterioriated areas of neighborhoods without destroying their integrity, and toward a greater reliance on rehabilitating basically sound structures. These policies could be carried out without participation, of course, but consultation has proved to be invaluable in planning intelligently for the location of these units. Further, we would not have been able to implement such concepts without a generally enthusiastic reception within neighborhoods. And even with the increased effort this kind of development makes necessary, we have still begun a record number of middle- and low-income housing units. This does not mean that construction of larger developments has been completely abandoned but that in essentially stable neighborhoods it is sheer folly to ignore the desires of residents by insisting on grandiose and inappropriate planning. To put it as bluntly as possible, in a large number of cases neighborhood residents are right in their concerns and city policy has been wrong.

We have seen, moreover, that participation has resulted in far more effective programs. The Community Development Agency has instituted a number of programs tailored specifically to neighborhood needs. For example, twenty-two Maternal and Infant Care Centers have been established in areas where some expectant mothers rarely see a doctor during their pregnancies; these neighborhoods have an infant mortality rate higher than that in almost any Western nation. In the three years the centers have been in operation the infant mortality rate has dropped substantially—and the centers deserve most of the credit.

Similarly, legal-service programs run out of neighborhoods with substantial guidance from within the communities has sharply increased the number of people using these services. As with the neighborhood city halls in middle-income neighborhoods, the legal-services program answers a specific need—lack of money to hire a lawyer to settle legal grievances. All these projects have given neighborhoods something they never had before—a sense that they have access to the system in such important areas as legal, health, and housing services.

I have spoken throughout this chapter of the kind of planning that affects poor neighborhoods, largely because it was in these neighborhoods that alienation from the city government was most intense and because our initial efforts to improve services were made where the demand was most critical.

But it is clear, at least from my experiences, that the disenchantment with the city government goes far beyond poor or black neighborhoods into every community, no matter how affluent. Indeed, as I have already noted, a major criticism of my administration has been that "Lindsay is doing too much for the poor" or, less delicately, "too much for the blacks."

This complaint arose, I think, not so much from a lack of our substantive efforts, for in terms of the key demands of middle-income communities—more police protection, better sanitation, improved transit, protection of recreational areas—our efforts were intense. Rather, I think they arose because of the visible signs of consultation and cooperation between the city and its poor communities. We had, I think, underestimated the depth of past communications failures and the consequent total disillusionment with the city's concern and capacity to care for its citizens.

For example, we believed we had planned an exciting program in community development in Brooklyn. Instead of ramming an elevated expressway through the middle of an established neighborhood, we proposed to build a road along existing railroad tracks in order to displace a minimum number of people. Further, we planned to use air rights above the road for schools and housing and open space—a joint-development (federal-state-city) idea that would have utilized federal highway money to build vitally important facilities. Former Secretary of Transportation Boyd was enthusiastic, as were many urban planners who were highly critical of conventional road-building plans. But the citizens of the affected neighborhoods did not want it. They fought it consistently, and ultimately the plan had to be abandoned. This is a case where, in my judgment, the "community" was wrong. But we learned that the community still has to govern, because the resentment and opposition would simply have been too great to enable the plan to be really effective. We had to be aware of this truth, like it or not.

The principle of participation is as valid in middle-income communities as in poor areas. It may even be easier to implement, since more affluent neighborhoods already have a number of established, articulate organizations and individuals and because they have greater experience in accomplishing their goals within bureaucratic institutions. We have tried to achieve this in a variety of ways—for example, by extending the task forces and police precinct councils into more affluent neighborhoods. My view is that instituting additional participatory programs, particularly neighborhood city halls, in these communities will offer real hope for the alleviation of disaffection that has been so deep and so widespread.

The experiment to broaden the effective power of individuals over their government is far from over. There remain many difficulties, and there will no doubt be continuing conflict, mistakes, and occasional failure. But I do not regret in the least my decision to run my administration as a partner in government, not as the master. It is easy—it is also tempting—to forget that the ultimate power in a free society is its people. History and tradition have put us a long way from the Jeffersonian credo that every man should become "an acting member of the common government," with a continuing responsibility for his community. But I believe this to be a valid goal today, and a critical achievement if we are to release ourselves from the sense of despair and hopelessness which is the legacy of the political past of our cities.

II

The Deeper Struggles

I HAVE SPOKEN *about some of the issues we have grappled with during my four years as Mayor of New York City. Some of them have particularly local application, but all of them are related to problems gripping other cities as well. And this, perhaps, is the most important lesson of my years as New York's Mayor—that while in many ways ours is a unique city, it also binds us to the other urban centers of America with a common set of problems and a common need for fundamental changes in the way we stand in relation to the state and federal governments.*

In this second section, I want to talk of the broader issues that touch on every big city—crime, poverty, the basic shortage of funds that make municipal services a steadily losing race against demands. Of necessity, I will draw on my experience in New York—that is the city I know—but many of the basic facts of city life are applicable elsewhere. Taken together, these facts pose a distinct national challenge. Either we shall face up to the work that must be done in our cities or we shall no longer have our cities as places of vitality in our society. And, given a nation with three-fourths of its population living in metropolitan areas, it is difficult to see how greatness will remain with a country that does not act to insure greatness in the centers where its people live and work.

There is no real chance here to touch on many of the

issues that are directly related to the quality of urban life. Urban planning, labor disputes, rent control, the multiple problems in urban school systems, preservation of city land for mixed uses, specific management improvements in city services—all of these are concerns that any effective city government must keep in mind, and responsible discussion of any of these subjects would require another book. But as important as they may be, they cannot match the urgency of basic issues affecting our cities: crime, poverty, and relations with state and federal governments. It is this set of issues that dominates urban America today—and it is this set of issues that must be swiftly, effectively resolved.

VII

The Pervasive Dilemma: I—Poverty and the Welfare Trap

PARTICIPATION AND communication are essential tools for untangling our cities' problems. But we also need a much deeper substantive understanding of the most important, most malignant sores to see how and why they have infected the city and how their growth can be arrested. We need to appreciate thoroughly the ways in which many current public programs and policies not only fail to solve the problems they attack, but actually compound them. There are many examples: physical decay, congestion, and the housing and transportation programs intended to combat them; failures to deliver essential services like health; and the outmoded, Byzantine government structures that cannot deliver effectively.

I have already discussed some of these in this book. Two of these problems, however, deserve special attention. Both of them tend to polarize the city, splitting race from race and class from class. Both of them breed myths and simplistic responses, diverting citizens from an honest search for solutions. Both of them offer visible platforms from which bigoted, dangerous political appeals can be made.

One of these areas is crime, which I shall discuss in the next chapter. The other is the two-sided dilemma of poverty and the welfare system. In each area, we desperately need to dispel some popular misconceptions and to dispassionately assess the improvements within our powers. Until now, many of us have tended to be defensive, to argue that simple solutions proposed for political purposes are wrong and destructive. Those of us in city government must also demonstrate that we can effect constructive, far-reaching reforms, policies that can in fact help our efforts to ease poverty and lawlessness. For without effective programs we can expect many to turn, in frustration and confusion, to myopic answers that will only make our problems worse.

Earlier I discussed the frequent walks I take through the streets of New York, through the diverse neighborhoods of this city. Sometimes my walks encourage me, as I watch a community refurbishing a block on its own or creating a vest-pocket park on a lot formerly cluttered with rubble and garbage. Sometimes they underscore some failures of the city government—streets where abandoned cars rust in unattended blight or where sanitation service has been inadequate. Sometimes I'm also reminded of past failures still complicating our tasks, when we pass potholes caused by poor paving thirty years ago or faulty or nonexistent sewer facilities in Queens or Staten Island, the products of earlier mistakes in planning, design, and construction—or, indeed, products of a total failure to plan or design or construct.

And then there are the walks through those parts of

the city that leave me in rage and despair, that raise profound questions, despite all our efforts and achievements, of whether we are locked in a struggle that simply cannot be won.

Those are my moods when I walk through a neighborhood like Brownsville, a community in central Brooklyn that was once a Jewish residential neighborhood and is now almost exclusively black and Puerto Rican. We think that about 100,000 people live in Brownsville, but nobody really knows the exact number. Even with all our governmental records and surveys, more than 20 per cent of Brownsville residents escape official recognition. Many work sporadically, if at all, and have no permanent address nor any connection with public agencies. We simply do not know who they are.

But we do know about those we can locate. Their average annual income is little more than half the city average—an overall average that itself reflects the incomes of many other poor whites, blacks, and Puerto Ricans. Not a single census tract in Brownsville has median income near middle-class levels. Of almost 50,000 housing units in the area, about 4 per cent are standard. The remaining 96 per cent are all substandard, decaying below the barest levels of adequacy.

By some other statistical measures Brownsville ranks very high. More of its infants die at birth than in any other community in New York. More of its young people are delinquents. More of its citizens are the victims of crime. By every index we use to measure the suffering of a community—narcotics addiction, welfare dependency, sickness, and malnutrition—Brownsville leads all other city neighborhoods.

And those bloodless numbers do not exaggerate the reality of life in Brownsville. Its residents grow accustomed to the littered streets, the homes without water, the scrabbling sound of rats' feet. Its abandoned buildings sag in vacant lines, the tin in their windows staring harshly over the sidewalks. Weathered men sit emptily on porch stoops, and four small children sleep tangled, sharing a single lumpy mattress.

A hard-boiled newsman writes: "Animals in the zoo live better than this. Zoos are heated and kept clean."

A local pastor observes bitterly: "If there is a hell, the people of Brownsville will take it in stride."

This is a brief portrait of one New York City neighborhood. It is also a microcosmic portrait of a nation within America, an isolated world taking fragmented shape in Chicago and Detroit, Newark and St. Louis, Atlanta and Washington and Los Angeles.

Of those we can count in that hidden nation, a million are jobless or working at subsistence wages. At least 4 million live in poverty. About a million housing units are substandard.

It is a nation with infant mortality rates 60 per cent higher than the rest of the country's, with maternal mortality rates three and four times as high. Its schools do not teach and its children do not learn. Its residents are victims of crime five to forty times as frequently as other Americans.

It is a nation offering its citizens no evidence that their lives will improve.

And this nation touches us all. It is reaching into

smaller cities, only recently discovering the problems of persistent poverty, substandard housing, and inadequate municipal services. It is spreading into suburban neighborhoods like those around New York City, where the incidence of welfare and crime is increasing more rapidly than in the central city. In 1967, for instance, one-fifth of America's black urban poor lived in the suburbs, and more than one-quarter of suburban blacks lived in poverty.

In other words, all of us confront the consequences of pervasive poverty in America. We cannot escape them. One flees the central city in vain, for the problems follow. One-fourth of the civil disorders that rocked America during 1967 occurred in communities with populations under 50,000. Some of the worst startled such apparently tranquil suburbs as Plainfield, New Jersey.

If the "other America" was once invisible, it is so no longer. Surely, after the summers and springs we have endured, after the violent disorders and militant demonstrations, after the quiet evidence of statistics has accumulated, we must recognize that we face the most severe challenge to the promise and progress of this country since the Depression.

And still, many of us—men and women of good will and decent instincts—continue to disregard what we see before us.

I remember walking through Brownsville and East New York in September 1967 with four prominent businessmen, men supposedly grounded in the reality of the world around them.

There was the late Gerald Phillippe, president of General Electric. All he said was, "Unbelievable."

There was Gilbert Fitzhugh, chairman of Metropolitan Life. "It makes you heartsick," he said. "You don't know where to start, but you know something has to be done."

There was J. Irwin Miller, chairman of the Cummins Engine Company in Columbus, Indiana. "The number-one problem of the country," this industrialist told me, "is the big city. There is no issue of greater danger to this nation."

These men were hardly militants. Like the members of the President's Commission on Civil Disorders, they were moderate, prudent men who were shocked by the tragedy of what they saw. With them, each of us—and particularly those who hold a political trust from our citizens—must admit that the tragedy exists and determine to end it.

And that will be only the beginning. Once determined to act, many of us will tend simply to assume that present methods of dealing with poverty are appropriate and rational, that sudden shifts in our policies would somehow be imprudent, impractical, or wrong. But we must not succumb to that laziness of spirit or failure of imagination. In addition to admitting the existence of poverty, it is urgent that we understand the futility of our present efforts to confront it. We must realize that our present policies are vacuous and dangerously unresponsive. Their failures are not merely that they fall short of ending the problem. Far worse, they make the problem infinitely worse. They insure further poverty and further hopelessness among the poor. They guarantee continued waste of the monies we spend on the problem and growing bitterness among the decent, hard-working Americans whose tax dollars are spent with no evidence of meaningful progress. When expensive policies fail by the standards both of the helped and those helping, polarization and resentment are inevitable.

In short, we cannot continue our present course. All of us must recognize the existence of a separate nation of the poor in the hearts of our cities. All of us must determine to end that poverty with rational, effective, just, and humane policies. And all of us must seek to fundamentally change the level and direction of our current efforts to aid the poor.

Most immediately, we must reform the existing welfare system, for it wastes more money, compounds the problems more seriously, and produces greater bitterness than all the rest of our efforts to cure poverty combined. To understand why the welfare system has failed, and how it must be changed, we need to examine more carefully the sources of poverty in New York and other cities and the ways in which welfare not only fails to eliminate these causes but actually strengthens their effects.

In New York City last year, about 1.2 million residents—about 15 per cent of the city's population—lived in poverty. Why are they poor?

The first part of the answer lies in the reasons they live in New York in the first place, and how they got there. Two-fifths of the poor in New York are black and another third are Puerto Rican. Most of those minority poor are recent migrants to New York or are the children of recent migrants.

In particular, many of the blacks living in New York migrated from the South during the past twenty-five years. Immediately following World War II, a revolution swept across the farms of the southern United States that effectively eliminated the demand for black farm workers. In twenty Mississippi Delta counties, for instance, the employment of unskilled farm workers dropped by 90 per cent in the space of five short years from 1949 to 1954.

Because there were no other opportunities for unskilled blacks in the South, they left for the "promised land" in the North. Unlike all the previous spurts of black migration to the North, this movement was not caused by the lure of available jobs in northern cities, but by the disappearance of jobs in the South. When the migrants arrived in New York and other cities, there were few jobs available for them.

And the reasons for the paucity of available jobs constitute the second half of the explanation of poverty.

To begin with, the migrants and their children have few skills—since they are the products of inadequate educational systems—in a labor market increasingly dominated by the demand for skilled labor. Further, as the migrants moved into the central-city ghettos—the only areas in which they were able to find housing—many jobs were moving out of the central cities into the suburbs. Further still, many blacks and Puerto Ricans have been trapped in the diminishing pockets of unskilled jobs by racial discrimination. And finally, the extremely low wages of those jobs to which the migrants have been confined have convinced many of them that their labor has no value and that they will never be able to climb the occupational ladder to more lucrative, less demeaning employment. Indeed, one would expect that from the city's labor market, in which about one-third of the jobs—1.1 million in all—pay less than $90 a week.

For all those reasons and more, over a million New Yorkers live in poverty. Having steadily limited their opportunities in employment, society has proffered the welfare system instead. But rather than curing those two central causes of poverty in our northern cities, the welfare system exacerbates them.

To understand this tragedy, we must take a close look at how welfare operates. In New York and other cities, welfare is a collection of programs offering public assistance to those who cannot support themselves. Some of the programs do not normally cause contention: aid to the aged, the blind, and the disabled; veterans' assistance; and general assistance for the destitute. Nearly half of New York's welfare budget goes to such cases, whose needs are accepted and whose support causes no resentment.

It is the other half of the welfare system that causes controversy and bitterness among taxpayer and recipient alike, the half to which people refer when they snarl about "welfare"—the program known as AFDC: Aid to Families with Dependent Children. It is the program through which the government assists needy families where the father is missing, or has deserted, and where the children require full-time care, preventing the mother from finding work.

It is AFDC that, although born as a system of temporary relief for families whose breadwinner was put out of work by the Depression, has become the principal method of assisting the poor in America. By the time this book is published, between 6 and 7 million mothers and children will be receiving AFDC throughout the country, at an annual cost of more than $3 billion, slightly more than half of it borne by the federal government. New York City alone accounts for about 10 per cent of those recipients. And, as the heart of the welfare system, AFDC is the program that so fundamentally fails to cure the causes of urban poverty.

The first major cause of the terrible concentration of the poor in urban ghettos was that many were forced to flee the South, unable to subsist there. The AFDC system has played an important part in sustaining that movement. Because the system permits nearly total discretion to state welfare agencies, the poor in penurious southern states have literally been unable to survive.

Even today, for example, Mississippi tells a family of six that they must live on $55 a month: for food, shelter, clothing, medical needs, the total cost of survival. The child of a Mississippi family is supposed to be able to subsist on thirty cents a day.

Though not quite so extreme, the same kind of starvation grants are offered in most other southern states. That in itself would be enough to force the poor to flee the South. But when one adds the broad powers given to state welfare officials—the powers almost arbitrarily to deny assistance to those in need, to pry needlessly into the details of a poor woman's life—one wonders how any poor have remained in some states. Our federally enacted system, with its localized grants of authority, has virtually mandated the movement of many of the nation's poor into its north-central cities.

Compounding that pressure, the federal system pays most of the costs of the inadequate southern assistance programs and much smaller proportions of the increasingly heavy burden of relief in the northern urban states. Mississippi receives 84 per cent of its AFDC budget from Washington, while New York receives only 50 per cent. The eight largest northern states bear 73 per cent of local and state AFDC costs, although they include only 46 per cent of the nation's population. And as the burden of paying for welfare continues to grow, northern cities like New York must scrimp on other absolutely crucial services.

Unfortunately, one of the barriers to reform of this disastrous regional inequity in the AFDC system is the prevalence of some common beliefs about those fleeing the South. Many think that migrants come to cities like New York specifically "to get on welfare," to take advantage of relatively more generous grant levels in the northern states. And thus many people resist the urgency of easing the welfare burdens of northern cities.

That might be a reasonable argument, except that the belief on which it is based simply isn't true. Every study made in New York tells us that the overwhelming majority of AFDC recipients have lived in the city at least two years before they join the rolls, and that only 2 per cent have lived here less than a year. In fact, families flee to New York to look for jobs, not welfare. Many of them struggle in jobs that do not pay enough to provide subsistence for their families; out of economic necessity and the hopeless lack of real employment opportunity, some of the families turn to welfare as their only alternative. And those with few skills and poor education obviously have fewer decent employment opportunities. Here, too, far from helping solve this problem, the welfare system compounds it.

How is this done? First, welfare provides for little real job training. Despite the existence of a dozen federal manpower programs, none of them is directly tied into the welfare system, where those most in need of jobs are trapped. The welfare caseworker spends hours filling out forms but almost no time teaching job skills to those who want to work or finding employment for those who could work at paraprofessional jobs such as nurses' and teachers' aides. Further, most cities are unable to use welfare funds to supplement the incomes of the paraprofessionals who are at the lowest levels so that they will be encouraged to stay on their jobs and develop the skills they need for more responsible employment.

Second, until this year AFDC directly discouraged employment by providing that a dollar of welfare benefits would be lost for every additional dollar earned from a job. That amounted to a 100 per cent tax on earnings; no matter how hard a welfare recipient with a large family worked on a job, his total disposable family income would not increase. Not surprisingly, many workers decided that full-time work at menial jobs offering no hope of advancement were hardly worth the effort, particularly when their families' income would be increased if they deserted and thus enabled their wives to go on welfare.

Third, the AFDC welfare system creates a set of inducements whose effect has been to further undermine the self-respect of the unskilled male worker. In any case, he would have trouble retaining his self-respect in a labor market that increasingly tended to consider his skills out of date, but the federal welfare system has intensified the problem by refusing to provide financial support for a family headed by a male working full time at wages too low to provide full family support. The one way for him to provide adequately for his wife and family is to technically desert them so that his wife can qualify for AFDC; then he surreptitiously provides her with some of his own job earnings. The net effect, of course, is to deny the low-wage worker the chance to maintain his integrity with his family, to imply to him that his failure to earn high wages stamps him as part of an underclass, to pose for him the impossible choice of deserting his family to provide them more adequate support or remaining with them at a considerably lower standard of living. Only in a few states, including New York with its Home Relief Program for family cases, are the families of the working poor offered income supplementation. And the federal government does not reimburse those states with a program for the working poor; New York City and New York State must bear the full financial burden of their Home Relief Program.

Fourth, because the federal government does not yet support supplementation for the working poor, states and localities cannot afford less than a 10 per cent tax on the employment earnings of the working poor. A man earning $3,500 by working full time might be able to receive an extra $1,200 from Home Relief in New York City to help support his wife and two children, but if he worked steadily and was promoted to a job paying $4,500, his income would not increase. The incentive for him to improve himself on his job is obviously weakened.

Generally, the welfare system compounds the problem of inadequate employment opportunities by saying to the recipients: "Here, since you've failed to provide for yourself, take a small stipend. But don't try to save, don't try to work, don't try to make yourself something better than you are." The welfare system has succeeded in promoting a permanent underclass, vast numbers of permanent wards of the state.

The history of AFDC helps explain the program's shortcomings, for when it began, during the depths of the Depression, it was intended for widows and the families of permanently disabled men. It was not designed to help huge numbers of the urban poor. Whatever its origins, however, we can no longer treat so vast a group of Americans as economic cripples, assuming through the system we perpetuate that they are incapable of work and that there is no work for them. A system that assumes this about some of its people has no place in a civilized society, which, as defined by Jane Addams, is one that reflects "an attitude of equal respect in all men." For by telling the urban poor that there is no place for them, no way in which they can support themselves and their children in pride and dignity, we have denied them equal respect. Such a system must clearly be scrapped.

But, once again, a common belief about welfare clients helps prevent the reform of these inhuman features of the welfare system: the conventional notion that welfare rolls teem with chiselers who soak the city's taxpayers for all they're worth. I can only invite those who still believe that to join me in the city's streets someday and talk with those on welfare. They would discover that under the recent limits imposed by the state legislature, a child on welfare in New York is supposed to be fed on sixty-six cents a day; that a family is supposed to pay for clothing and furniture with a share of a grant amounting to less than $100; that the system regards a telephone as a luxury and provides absolutely nothing for recreation and entertainment. How many would regard that kind of sustenance as a prize to be wrested from the taxpayers? Various groups of middle-class suburban families, in fact, have tried to subsist on welfare-grant levels for a week and found it impossible—and they knew that within a week their self-imposed poverty would end.

No, the poor hardly cheat by pretending they can't work in order to be eligible for the "luxury" of receiving welfare. If they do cheat, they cheat the other way—for example, a woman will take a part-time or full-time job and try to hide it so that she can still retain her full welfare benefits. The way to combat such "cheating" is not to shackle welfare recipients with intimidating sets of regulations, but to provide them with an effective incentive system under which they can try to find decent jobs without sacrificing their capacity to care for their children.

And that is what they want. According to the recent survey, seven out of ten welfare mothers in New York said they would rather work than continue on welfare. And two of the remaining three said they would prefer work if their children could be attended during the day. One mother, divorced and with three children, apparently reflected a general feeling: "I know," she said, "that being on welfare might guarantee a roof over your head, but at a price of practically everything that is necessary for a person's confidence and self-respect."

Whenever I hear these myths about the poor flocking to New York for the glamorous "easy life" on the welfare rolls, I vividly recall an experience I had one day when I took a prominent national figure with me through one of the city's worst neighborhoods. We walked down a street that looked as though it had been bombed. We entered an apartment building so dilapidated that we assumed it must be abandoned. But it wasn't. Families were trying to live there. We spoke with one woman, the mother of four children. She had tried to find work, she said, but couldn't, and she couldn't find care for her children, since the day-care units in her neighborhood had long waiting lists. She received welfare, but she had enough for meat only once or twice a month.

My companion looked around the apartment and asked her, "Why did you come to New York?"

"To find a better life," she said.

He looked around again, a little startled.

"Did you find it?" he asked finally.

She answered simply, "Yes I did."

For all these reasons it seems to me absolutely imperative that we change this system immediately. We must recognize that the entire approach of the welfare system has failed, that it has exacerbated the causes of urban poverty, helped institutionalize dependency, and severely and inequitably burdened state and local budgets. It should be completely junked for something better.

A new program should have four basic features:

1. It should provide a national income-maintenance program, with national standards adjusted for regional

cost-of-living differences. It should also provide a decent income level for those who cannot support themselves and their families. And it should be fully funded by the federal government so that urban taxpayers are not forced to pay for national problems.

2. It should totally separate the task of providing income support from that of providing social services. At present, the welfare system imposes so many national rules and regulations that it is strangling itself in red tape. The administrative costs of the system are as high as those of the entire Internal Revenue Service, which handles twenty times the money. Those services that are in fact needed—assistance in health, housing, and employment—should be locally directed and totally separated from the entirely different function of keeping needy families alive.

3. A new system should actively encourage recipients to work by providing incentives to work instead of imposing a dollar-for-dollar tax on all earnings of welfare families.

4. Perhaps most important, we need an integration between the need for support and the possibilities for employment, a system channeling those receiving support directly into meaningful job opportunities.

In New York there is an especially urgent need for a new system because we are desperate for workers in almost every kind of service institution. Those on welfare with adequate incentives and support could provide this man- and womanpower. With the right kind of system, we could multiply a hundred times over our present training program, providing, for example, hundreds more technical aides in many services while maintaining their incomes. In many cases we could train registered nurses by starting women without skills at the nurse's-aide level and providing training as they work on their jobs.

With an income-support system tied to job training, we would open the door to self-sufficiency for our poor communities. Higher incomes would allow the poor to live with dignity and at the same time would lower the burden on the public of providing services to those without the means of self-support. That seems a goal worthy of the effort it will require to redesign the federal welfare system.

Pressures are building for the federal government to assume the leadership in this area, and the welfare reforms proposed by President Nixon are an important beginning. But far more must be done. The cities cannot wait for a reluctant Washington to act. Following the lead of forty other states (Massachusetts the most recent), New York State should relieve all the cities and counties of the state of the cost of welfare. The reasons for national takeover also apply for state takeover, and New York now lags behind most of the other states of the nation in this respect.

Meanwhile, in New York City we have been making our own moves to replace the current system. In the past three years we have adopted several key reforms that are beginning to point the way to a better system.

First, New York City has been pioneering in the separation of income maintenance from social service, and others are beginning to follow. We have adopted a system of simple declaration of need for support to replace the lengthy investigations that formerly took most of a caseworker's time.

Second, we also pioneered in providing real incentives

for employment through our Employment Incentive Program, which has now been adopted as part of federal policy. Under this program, the AFDC recipient has been allowed to keep the first $85 of employment earnings each month without tax, plus one-third of the remaining salary, in addition to welfare benefits. Through EIP, we have been encouraging recipients to be trained, to obtain and retain jobs, and to increase their earnings through employment, for through EIP, finally, they can indeed raise their income by working. Since this program was instituted, more than 25,000 people in welfare families have participated—and some genuine success has been won in helping families leave welfare for self-sustaining jobs.

Third, the city's Manpower and Career Development Agency is in the process of opening regional manpower centers throughout the city in which the unskilled will receive intensive training for available jobs. We intend to feed as many welfare recipients into the centers' skill-training courses as we can. And we hope that those industries in New York which must bear some of the welfare burden through their taxes will help themselves by hiring from this pool of newly trained talent.

Finally, we have designed a new, radically different program to improve the earnings of low-income workers at the lowest possible cost to the city. The program is called the Training Incentive Payments Program, for which the city received funds early in the summer of 1969 from the federal government for a pilot test. Under TIPP an employer would train low-income workers by any method he felt would best equip them for the jobs he needed to fill. If the worker's salary were raised, the city would reimburse the employer for the costs of the training, based on a proportion of the increase in earnings.

The program would not involve high-risk, expensive institutional training without the guarantee of success, for payments would be made only if and when a worker's wages were actually increased. There would be no new government bureaucracy, for the employer would choose his own methods of training. And there would be no training for jobs that don't exist because the employer would train people only for jobs that already needed to be filled. There is no question that job openings exist—about 40,000 well-paying jobs now go unfilled because employers cannot find workers with adequate skills. Under TIPP employers will be able to train low-skilled workers and, if the training produces the necessary skills, promise them wage advancements without risk; those assurances should induce unskilled workers previously without hope of improvement to stay on the job.

With federal support, we hope that the Training Incentive Payments Program will help fill job openings, increase the salaries of low-income workers, and provide them with incentives to continue improving their skills. If it does succeed, we will be reducing an ever-increasing pool of potential welfare recipients.

All these efforts have been designed to improve the welfare system. Ultimately, however, welfare remains a program dependent on federal and state policy for direction. Neither the cities nor the states can by themselves erase the legacies of national economic conditions. They particularly cannot shoulder the system's financial burdens or the social dissension that its failures induce.

The federal government must, therefore, assume the full financial costs of an improved system. No one else can. Federal failure to provide employment and to impose uniform minimum-welfare standards on the local level have caused the impossible problems with which too many cities have been grappling in recent years.

Such a federally financed system would solve much of the problem, but the final, most fundamental change comes less easily. We must admit our failures and start anew. We must create not just a program; we must even dare to hope for an entirely different set of social attitudes, which will extend opportunity to those we now regard as cripples. A new program can help provide income, protect dignity, encourage work, and end the disgrace of dependency. But only a new attitude can offer to both the poor and our cities an alternative to increasing bitterness, to the mutual suspicions that so complicate our tasks ahead.

VIII

The Pervasive Dilemma: II—Crime

"THE LAND IS FULL of bloody crimes and the city is full of violence." So spoke the Lord to Ezekiel. That vision is still with us; so is all of the danger of crime: the threat to the property, the safety, and the lives of our people; the danger of racial and ethnic polarization between groups who live close to each other but without communication; and the danger of fruitless attempts to resolve that problem by turning away from the historic traditions of America.

I think I reflect the feeling of every mayor in the country in saying that no issue is of more concern to the typical urban resident than crime: no issue brings forth more emotional demands, threatens the core of confidence in a community more seriously, or requires more urgent attention from us. In part this is because of the very nature of a criminal act. No set of statistics, no program, however impressive, can resolve the grievance of a man whose home was burglarized, whose property was stolen, whose wife was assaulted, whose children were attacked by criminals. No plea to examine causes and alternatives can really answer the complaints of a neighborhood whose residents are afraid to walk through the streets of their community.

Indeed, beyond all the cost of crime, beyond the $20 billion a year, nationally, and the untold resources diverted from urgent services into police protection, courts, and the jails, the key cost of crime is what it does to us as individuals and as members of a community. It puts us behind the locked doors of our homes and apartments and turns nighttime in the city into a time of fear. It makes us suspicious of others, and often makes us suspicious of anyone whose skin color is different from our own. It in effect wipes away our legal right to move freely, to assemble, and to use our environment with any confidence. In the words of the president of the American Bar Association, "Fear of random attack imprisons us as surely as any Berlin wall." And if for no other reason than to restore a sense of personal freedom and security, crime is the number-one domestic enemy of the city, and it must be treated as such.

The crime rate in large American cities has been almost twice as great as the national average; and in the biggest of our cities, those over a million, it has been more than double the average and almost triple the suburban rate. There are signs that this is beginning to change, to the extent that suburban crime rates are beginning to match, and in some cases now exceed, those of the central cities. Even though much of this rate is attributable to factors other than a sign of generally greater lawlessness —the sharp jump in the number of low-income youths in cities and improved crime-reporting figures are the two basic reasons for the constant upsurge in crime figures—it does not change the fact that there *is* more crime today in all of our cities.

Nor is it an answer to the demand for better protection to demonstrate that the fear of crime has always been with us—although that is certainly true. A Senate investigating commitee found that "the cost of crime is steadily advancing . . . the administration of justice has broken down"—and that was in 1933. The *New Republic* charged that "the administration of criminal justice has completely broken down"—and that was in 1925. *Harper's Magazine* described the crime increase as an event that "shocked the universal conscience"—and that was in 1852.

The persistence of this issue, however, makes response no less urgent, particularly today when concern about crime has in many areas become an obsessive fear and when irresponsible people promise swift and false solutions by abandoning fundamental freedoms. It means instead that all of us—police, citizens, public officials—must be willing to undertake the long, hard work of really engaging in crime prevention and control.

This work has, I think, three basic elements: first, an understanding of how and why crime occurs; second, a willingness to understand those solutions that will not work and that promise only a betrayal of the American heritage without offering any real hope of increased security; third, an all-out effort to implement those programs and policies that can in fact offer a chance of reversing the spread of crime.

One of the most unjustified myths at large in our cities is that the black ghetto areas of the city are staging areas for criminals and that most of the residents there are somehow sympathetic to lawlessness. In fact, there is nothing that unites every neighborhood of the city, black and white, affluent, middle class, and poor, more than a common demand for increased efforts against crime. Indeed, in one poll taken in New York City two years ago among residents of a black neighborhood, the number-one demand, despite all the complaints about housing, health, and poverty, was for *more* police protection. The reason is not hard to understand. Crime is far more of a danger in the poor neighborhoods of a city than anywhere else. The President's Crime Commission found that residents in such neighborhoods were three to ten times more likely to become the victims of a violent crime than other city dwellers; a study in one large city confirmed this finding and in fact revealed that the danger was more than thirty times as great in a poor neighborhood than in an upper-income urban neighborhood.

This is a critical finding, for one of the principal dangers of crime in the cities is just this danger of racial and economic polarization. If white residents of the city regard black neighborhoods as essentially crime-prone, if they fail to understand how deeply black neighborhoods themselves fear crime, then stereotyping is an inevitable result. Similarly, if black residents of the city do not recognize the distinction between racism and a legitimate, real, substantial fear of crime, they are likely to conclude that there is no hope for overcoming racial distinctions, and the prospects for cooperation will be diminished.

This is one element of understanding. Even more urgent is the need to understand those remedies and proposals that do *not* work in curbing crime and disorder, that actually increase the danger of innocent bloodshed as well as dangers to the Republic. I want to give special emphasis to this point, for only if we understand what should not be done can we recognize those steps that can and have been effective.

The issue is *not* whether or not to combat crime with the full resources of the city. What is dividing Americans from one another is the diagnosis and remedy too many of us seem ready to apply.

Many have come to be enthralled by simplistic solutions which promise, but cannot deliver, a speedy end to crime; which proclaim that a greater use of naked force will restore domestic peace; and which hold that we can guarantee the safety of our future by denying the lessons of the past and the heritage of the Bill of Rights. We would face a terrifying dilemma if these assumptions really reflected the truth. We might then have to choose between the random terror of the criminal and the official terror of the state. We might then have to concede, openly and candidly, that the Great Experiment in free government died, the victim of violence, before its two-hundredth birthday.

But we need make no such concession. For all the certainty of those who preach repression, it will never be an effective weapon in the battle against crime and violence. At best it can only be a temporary sedative for the fear that disorder breeds. The real struggle will be longer and harder. It will require compassion and patience as well as determination and effort. It requires, also, the public's recognition that Supreme Court decisions, refusal to shoot petty criminals, and freedom of peaceful assembly are *not* responsible for the growth of crime and violence.

Does it help, for example, to gun down a thirteen-year-old boy because he was looting a store? The men who run our police forces, the men who bear the brunt of the fight against crime, do not seem to think so. According to a survey by the International Association of Chiefs of Police, the overwhelming majority of ranking officers in cities that were hit by rioting in the spring of 1968 believe that deadly force should be used only as a last resort—in the face of a direct, immediate threat to life.

The same thought was echoed by line patrolmen who were interviewed. "When you start to shoot," one said, "you can lose control very quickly. You have to suppress your emotions." "No sane policeman would shoot unless he received orders," said another.

These police opinions reflect more than compassion; they reflect a strong belief that more force would only spawn more violence; that more innocent lives, both police and civilian, would be lost; and that the overriding goal of restoring order in the streets would be lost.

This was one of the major lessons of the bloody summer of 1967. It was one of the major findings of the Commission on Civil Disorders. And it is a lesson that should be learned by those who seek political support by preaching to the baser instincts now abroad in this nation. We know what *will* work: rapid deployment of enough police, swift dispersal of crowds, isolation and detention of troublemakers, calm determination to restore order. We saw the truth of this in New York City during the tense days in East New York in 1966. The police, goaded and taunted, acted to disperse crowds and preserve order, but not a shot was fired. The officers had been told, through the chain of command, to fire only when in actual danger. In the words of a newspaper decidedly unfriendly to police restraint, "Even the police veterans realized . . . that the seemingly dangerous gambit paid off. There were few casualties; the situation at all times was under control."

These are the techniques that police around the country have used successfully to control outbreaks of trouble. It is the kind of training we must encourage if the beginning of disorder is not to crest into a violent, bloody conclusion.

We are told, too, by self-announced experts, that the courts are coddling criminals; that the rights of suspects are being placed above those of society; and that, as a result, the crime rate is increasing.

What are the facts? Since the *Miranda* v. *Arizona* decision—which requires police to inform suspects of their constitutional rights before questioning them—we have had two exhaustive studies on the decision's effect. Both of these studies, conducted in two large cities, have come to the same conclusion: there has been no discernible effect on the conviction rate. Either suspects have confessed to crimes anyway or the police had enough evidence to convict without a confession.

The policeman's real handicap is not the fact that courts today are implementing the Bill of Rights, but that he is restricted by archaic structures and technology. The capacity to deal effectively with more crime lies not in force or deception but in new tools and more funds. I want to discuss this at some length later, in illustrating which techniques can work. The point here is that by focusing on court decisions rather than on the administration of justice and police operations, many commentators are simply ignoring the genuine impediments to effective police performance.

And while it is true that the national crime rate has increased since recent controversial court decisions, it was also increasing years before these decisions were handed down—it was, in fact, up 63 per cent in the 1950's as against the 1940's. It has been increasing because of the complex pressures and forces that drive men to crime, not because the Supreme Court is enforcing the Constitution.

There is much, then, that is simply irrelevant in today's frantic calls for repression. There is also something dangerous. For what happens if we begin to yield to this kind of demand for "law and order"? What happens if Supreme Court decisions are overturned, if police are ordered to arrest without any restraints on their conduct, if peace officers are ordered to shoot a looting thirteen-year-old? What happens if, after this victory for "law and order," we find—as we will—that the crime rate is still going up, that the streets are still not safe, that more and more lives have been lost, and that America is being divided into armed camps?

The answer, I am afraid, is that these defeated hopes for tranquillity will escalate into new and more dangerous demands. We see now the unfulfilled promises of another kind. In our deprived neighborhoods today much of the strongest force behind the drift into insurrection has been the failure to meet expectations, which has caused many to simply abandon hope of peaceful progress. We might well see this process repeated among other Americans, who would call for further abrogation of fundamental legal rights in a last desperate attempt to win back an orderly society—much as a gambler hurls more and more money after his losses.

Perhaps some would then look at the criminal law and demand to know why we need a unanimous jury vote to convict a person of a crime. Why not declare a suspect guilty summarily if he refuses to testify? Why not cast aside the privilege between clients and lawyers, between confessors and priests? And why presume a man innocent until proven otherwise? If the police arrest someone, isn't he probably guilty anyway?

What all this suggests is an old truth that needs new affirmation: once the road to repression is taken, it is hard—very hard—to turn back. Each new loss of liberty, as it fails to bring instant peace, will bring forth a call for the abrogation of another right, until the most brilliant document ever conceived for the protection of individuals becomes a shell—and crime and violence continue. We have already seen this process at work in this country. Many citizens have begun to equate criminal acts and violent disorders with noisy but peaceful demonstrations in the streets. They have begun to assume that the exercise of a constitutional right is no different from a crime or a riot—if those exercising that right happen to dress in unorthodox fashion or hold disagreeable beliefs.

Certainly it is a matter of concern when Americans find the ordinary channels of discussion and decision so unresponsive that they feel forced to take their grievances to the streets. And surely some who demonstrate are thoroughly deplorable, seeking confrontation and hoping for a brutal response to win sympathy or gain an issue. That is why those who uphold the law must be wiser and calmer than those who seek to repudiate it. Violent suppression of those who use—and seek to abuse—constitutional rights will, in the end, only increase the likelihood of more disorder and more conflict. It was, after all, a mob that taunted, jeered, and physically provoked an armed force on our soil into what we now call the Boston Massacre—the British "overreaction" we now regard as an assault on ideas and freedom as much as on people.

I do not minimize the dilemma of preserving order in times of tension. In New York City we have had more than a quarter of a million people marching for and against the same controversial cause on the same day. We have made mistakes. We have had difficulties. But we have shown that a well-trained, efficient police force can protect both the rights of demonstrators and the peace of the city. Yet in spite of this evidence, many—influenced, I am convinced, by the belief that crime and disorder and dissent are part of the same fabric—argue that the only way to insure order in a city is to drastically restrict any and all demonstrations, peaceful and otherwise. What is next? Shall we suppress controversial newspapers? Shall we forget what history has always taught us: that those who suppress freedom always do so in the name of "law and order"?

We dare not forget this. Those of us who believe in this country must begin to speak in support of that law and that kind of order which have kept this a vital nation for almost two centuries.

The basic law of this land guarantees the right of free

speech and peaceful assembly, in times of tranquillity and of crisis.

The American legal order presumes a man innocent until he is proven guilty, and it insists that punishment be imposed in a court by judge and jury, not on the street or in a precinct house by armed officers.

The Constitution provides that the law shall be made and changed only by the elected representatives of the people, and not by those who take the law into their own hands.

Let us remember this heritage of law and order—and the heritage of liberty we have built for ourselves and our children. It is a framework and a foundation that has served us too well and too long to be destroyed now. Let us remember, too, what those in other systems have taught us by grim examples. When we are tempted by calls to place bayoneted soldiers every five feet and to run over nonviolent demonstrators, we should ask ourselves whether we have seen that kind of society before. And of course we have: in every tyranny that rules by brute force. Only recently in Prague we saw the fulfillment of this vision. There were bayoneted soldiers every few feet, and in the streets was the blood of young men—with long hair and strange clothes—who were killed protesting Communist tyranny operating under the cloak of law and order. If we ever begin abandoning our own structure of justice and civil order, they will be *our* tanks and *our* children.

We must never forget, then, in responding to the threat of crime, how long and how hard we have fought to develop a system of order and justice. For if we forget we will have security, and we will have order. What will be missing is the quality that sets the life of a free man so far above the life of a slave.

But to reject repression is not to advocate resignation or surrender to crime. It is the number-one enemy of the city, and it must be fought. But if not by the tactics of tyranny, then how?

The answer, I think, is to engage in a total mobilization of the resources of the city—buttressed by substantial financial assistance from state and federal governments—to build a total system of crime-fighting machinery in every phase of city life that affects personal safety, from the police force to the courts and the correctional institutions. For these are the institutions charged with the responsibility for deterring, preventing, and punishing crime and turning offenders into law-abiding citizens. And the fact is that in city after city these institutions are not working properly. They have been burdened by inadequate funds, antiquated structures, and a total failure to understand how they can and must work with each other to provide a common effort against crime.

Early in my administration we established the Criminal Justice Coordinating Council, drawing together representatives from the whole spectrum of crime fighting: the Police Department, district attorneys, the courts, correction and probationary systems, outside organizations involved in reforming criminal justice (such as the VERA Institute of Justice, a private organization devoted to reform of the criminal system), and social-action agencies. We determined that a total effort should be launched. We are a long way from success, but I believe nonetheless that we are well on the road to critical improvements throughout our crime-fighting machinery.

The first area of concern, clearly, is the Police Department. Quite apart from the pressures between peace officers and ghetto residents, or other issues affecting urban tensions, the job of the police first and fundamentally is to preserve peace by deterrence. But how does a single policeman protect even one block from mugging, robbery, and burglary when several thousand people live on that block? How can we hope to put enough policemen in all of the city's parks, in all of the city's neighborhoods? The harsh fact is that, pushed to its extreme, the call for more and more policemen is a call for municipal bankruptcy. For even with a force of 32,000, the largest of any city in the Western world, larger than the armies of many nations, we do not have enough men. If we were to hire enough policemen to cover every block in New York twenty-four hours a day, it would cost us, every year, $25 billion—four times the entire city budget! And it still would not halt crime.

Of course, sheer size multiplies all our problems. How can the theft of even valuable goods—typewriters, television sets, jewelry—be detected in a city of this size? How can the police trace every pawnshop, every illegal "fence" who sells stolen goods, every apartment where such goods may be kept for the personal use of the criminal? Not even a police force of a million could do that job. Three years ago a former police commissioner of New York asked, "How long can we afford to react to crime . . . by adding manpower? When will we have enough men? Thirty thousand? Forty thousand? . . . Instead [of further increases], we should seek to maximize the potential of the men we have."

In a lengthy study of police manpower from 1940 to 1964, the Police Department concluded: "Our real strength in terms of available manhours in 1964 is *less* than what it was in 1940. Two patrolmen in 1940 provided the same number of working manhours as are obtained from three patrolmen under current working conditions." Put even more sharply, although there were 8,000 more *police* on the force in 1964 than there were in 1940, the real strength of the department had decreased by an astonishing 34 per cent.

Why? Why would we get fewer hours of work from a force with 8,000 more men? To those with any experience in commerce or management, the answer is clear. During that period the working conditions of New York policemen had dramatically improved. Vacation time had risen 50 per cent; mealtime had doubled; the work week had been changed from six to five days. The policeman of 1940 worked 311 days a year; by 1964 he was working 234 days a year.

These changes were fully justified. They were a matter of offering a man in the most arduous and demanding job in the city an equitable working life. But it does suggest the futility of attempting to solve the crime problem solely through the addition of large numbers of men. In fact, simply to get back to the 1940 levels of manhours—simply to get the same total productivity out of the force—the city would have to hire at least 12,000 more police, at a cost each year of $150 million. We cannot absorb a 50 per cent jump in total police costs. Given the perennial budget gap we face, that kind of investment for that kind of return is simply unacceptable.

We sought, then, another route: the maximum use and deployment of the police forces we have, combined with needed manpower increases. And I believe the results thus far offer genuine promise.

We *did* hire more police—4,000 of them, bringing our force up to 32,000 men—because it is clear that a constant level of manpower is not good enough. But we also attempted to gain more effective use of the men we have, and that goal brought us face to face with an antiquated and irrational structure that crippled both the men on the force and the city's ability to fight crime.

Here is one simple example. More than 2,000 of our police, highly trained and taught to fight crime, held down desk jobs in police precincts and elsewhere. Because of an attitude that assumed that bureaucratic lines were sacrosanct, no one bothered to ask why clerical jobs could not be held by clerks, thus freeing police to use their training in the work of fighting crime. What we did, then, was to hire 2,000 civilians to work in police precincts, providing a variety of services from clerical and typing skills to greeting citizens who came into the precinct. This effort immediately put 2,000 officers on the street at a cost far lower to the city than the traditional answer of hiring 2,000 more police, because clerks do not earn as much as policemen. Moreover, this step had an additional benefit. In many of the city's precinct houses, the presence of civilians, usually people from the immediate neighborhood, helped to ease the stereotype of the police station as alien to the community.

This was a relatively easy and simple reform. But how

effectively was a policeman's time being used? Shockingly, we found that each time a policeman apprehended a law breaker, from traffic offender to suspected murderer, it inevitably involved him in a massive waste of his time. If a motorist pleaded not guilty to a speeding charge, the policeman would have to show up at traffic court and wait until his case was called—often a waste of several hours. If he arrested a suspected felon after 5:00 P.M., he would have to wait until the next morning to arraign his suspect, and perhaps lose hours either of working time or time he should have had to rest and to be with his family. And he always had to arraign the suspect at a courthouse, often far from his precinct house.

We have thus begun in New York City a series of steps to end the traditional of waste of one department's time through the practices of another's. Because the Criminal Justice Coordinating Council was able to bring together representatives from each of the law-enforcement departments, we were able to design with relative speed a number of reforms.

First we launched the Traffic Alert Program, under which an officer is summoned directly from his duties when—and only when—his case is within an hour of being called in the court. Otherwise, he is on his job, helping to combat crime. In the first year of this experiment, 50 per cent of time previously wasted has been saved, and so has 50 per cent of the taxpayers' money, which would otherwise be spent in somehow making up the lost manpower.

Then we instituted a program for twenty-four-hour arraignment in the criminal courts. Thus, if a man is arrested at night he can immediately be brought before a magistrate for the initial step in the criminal process, making it unnecessary for the policeman to wait for the case to be called. Once again, there are other important benefits. For the accused, twenty-four-hour arraignment means that he need not spend a night in jail once the process of prosecution has been started, a practice that often meant that innocent people were jailed because they could not be bailed out until arraignment the next morning.

In the Bronx we have begun an experiment in which suspects are arraigned before a magistrate who is actually in the precinct house. Thus, a police officer who makes an arrest can go directly back to headquarters, turn the suspect over to the judicial process, and return to his work almost immediately. In the first months of operation, we have saved hundreds of hours of police time in this one experiment, and we are hopeful that its extension will save us far more. Further, the presence of a magistrate in the precinct house means a measure of added protection for suspects, who are afforded the presence of a nonpolice agency.

More than fifty years ago, when policemen had no organization to bargain for them and no protection against arbitrary working conditions, the state legislature passed a law designed to protect them. It provided that three shifts, or platoons, of police would work the city—from 8:00 A.M. to 4:00 P.M., from 4:00 P.M. to midnight, and from midnight to 8:00 A.M. This law made sense in 1911, when it was passed. But by 1969 it had become a severe impediment to better police protection.

Criminals, unfortunately, did not accommodate themselves to the police schedules. Their work, particularly crimes of violence, was concentrated between the hours of 6:00 P.M. and 2:00 A.M.—almost half the violent crimes in New York occur in those hours. Yet, because of the 1911 law, we could not direct police strength at those hours. Our strategy was to add a fourth shift, or platoon, of police, assigning it to the hours from 6:00 P.M. to 2:00 A.M. To do this, however, we had to change the law.

Astonishingly, the city did not have the power to change this law—the state legislature, most of whose members did not live or work in New York, controlled that decision. And for eight years two mayors and three police commissioners had been urging the change. Finally, this year, because of a mounting concern about crime and because of our campaign to generate public support for this reform, we got the change through. It has given us the power to put 50 per cent more men on the street at night at almost no increased cost. It demonstrates convincingly, I think, that once a city stops taking the existing structure as a God-given requirement and begins to look into the hard questions of reform, it can produce important and valuable improvements in its crime-fighting capacity.

Reforms, like the fourth platoon, that increase the productivity of our force are important, but they cannot be expected to produce improvements in a vacuum. The force itself must be provided with the equipment and the resources to battle crime in the modern urban context. And this means far better equipment than they now have.

One of the critical links between police and the citizenry is rapid communications, and in this area New York City has made significant strides. With the cooperation of the New York Telephone Company, we instituted the first three-digit emergency phone number in the country. Any citizen, in an emergency, can dial 911 and receive instant contact with a police command in his borough. Through new computers, the request for help is telegraphed from the telephone desk to the dispatch center in less than a minute, and help is sent instantly. The computers simultaneously advise the dispatching officer of the number and location of the patrol units in the area—which are on some other call, which are free. This is the new SPRINT communications system. It provides the fastest dispatch system in the world, computerizing the rounds of patrol cars to match the incidence of crime and providing a critical breakthrough in protection. In addition, every foot patrolman on the beat is now being equipped with a walkie-talkie tied in to the same computer and dispatch system and available to summon help and report disturbances instantly.

Finally, we are seeking one other reform, still opposed by the Patrolmen's Benevolent Association, to increase police presence without additional costs. In many low-density residential neighborhoods the fact of police presence is a powerful deterrent to crimes against property. We believe that the use of one-man patrol cars in areas where property crimes are the chief acts of lawlessness would enable us to double police presence without taking other men from equally vital jobs.

One major city has already found this practice so successful it is making it the pattern of patrol. It has the endorsement of the presidential Crime Commission's task force on police. And our own experiments in two residential areas show that it results in no increased danger whatever to the policemen. We are hopeful that this reform, too, will be instituted in the near future.

What I have outlined thus far are reforms directly affecting the police force. But it is clear that the police are only one part of the effort to combat crime. Our court system, for example, needs a general overhaul, from the speed with which suspects are arraigned to the treatment of offenders once they have been convicted and sentenced. Here, too, the Criminal Justice Coordinating Council, with the invaluable support of the VERA Institute of Justice, has suggested important new possibilities.

The first is to remove from the criminal process those who do not belong there. Alcoholics, for example, account for as many as half of all arrests in large precincts. It is apparent, however, that this endless revolving door—from street to jail to street to jail again—is serving no one and results in a great waste of police manpower. We have established an experimental program to treat alcoholics outside the criminal process. Through a project centered on the Bowery—Manhattan's skid row—we are providing counseling, medical service, and long-term care for those who want to break their dependence. Once again, this effort is directly related to crime, because it takes the police force out of an area where they are spending much time to little effect, and redirecting them toward the crimes against people and property that are the greatest danger.

Perhaps most importantly, we are now engaged in a major series of experiments to find a way out of the nightmare of drug addiction, which accounts for perhaps half of all street crimes and burglaries. A man on hard narcotics will do almost anything to get his fix—and this means more thefts, more purse-snatchings and muggings, and more danger in the city. Through a series of experimental programs, ranging from psychiatric therapy to tests with Methadone, a chemical drug that provides a possible alternative to the agony of straight withdrawal from heroin, we hope to supply answers for a large-scale effort to combat addiction apart from the fruitless pattern of arrest after arrest.

The war on narcotics must be as great a national commitment as was the War on Poverty planned by President Kennedy and announced by President Johnson. Clearly, responsibility at the local level is primary, and New York City has tried to fulfill that responsibility. Four years ago when I was first elected, there was *one* city-run narcotics-treatment facility. There are more than fifty now. We created the first city agency with a mandate to concentrate exclusively on addiction: the Addiction Services Agency. It was this department that created the Phoenix Houses, a pioneering effort to take addicts and let them build their own rehabilitation, living and working together and exercising self-responsibility. We began an intensified police drive, more than doubling our Narcotics Bureau and making every one of our 32,000 police directly responsible for narcotics in their area.

But more must be done. And here, too, a national effort is critical. To begin with, we need help to control the flow of narcotics into the country. Opium does not grow in Brooklyn. It grows abroad and is smuggled into the city through a thriving drug traffic. The federal government alone has the authority to work with foreign governments and with its immigration and customs services to stem this flood of poison. Further, vital research into the nature and causes of addiction has been almost totally ignored by Washington, in spite of our great ignorance about this cancer. In addition, narcotics cannot be conquered without an attack on organized crime, which controls the business and which reaps great profit from narcotics. And without a specific federal commitment to break up the organized crime empires—interstate combines which now exist as securely as any major corporation—we will continue to be plagued by addiction.

Drug abuse is becoming an increasing concern to the middle-class family, whose children are turning in alarming numbers not just to marijuana but to such dangerous drugs as the amphetamines and powerful hallucinogens. In New York City we have tried to meet this problem at its root by organizing educational programs within the schools in which young people who have themselves used drugs speak to the issue with more honesty and more authority than a conventional adult spokesman who may know less about drugs than his audience and whose overstatements may wipe out his entire message. It is not true that marijuana will turn a clean-cut youth into a homicidal maniac, and our children know it. But they may *not* know about the real dangers of mind-affecting drugs—and they must be informed by those who can answer their questions straight. It seems clear, also, that at least part of the fascination with drugs is an effort to share a private or communal experience away from involvements that seem artificial or useless. And however much we may shake our heads at this genuinely dangerous flirtation with drugs, we might also be asking some hard questions about what is missing—about why the shared experience of a marijuana cigarette seems so much more attractive than the shared effort of working with children who need help.

Also, the city is determined to combat the single worst indictment of our criminal and penal system—the rate of recidivism, or repeat offenders. The statistics are appalling, for they show that two-thirds of youthful first offenders later commit more crimes, a shocking indication that our present efforts are neither rehabilitating nor deterring criminals. In addition, we are undertaking a program of genuine rehabilitation, using a wide range of facilities. Through a program jointly designed by the city and Robert Kennedy, we are bringing VISTA and Teacher Corps personnel into correctional institutions to prepare young offenders for their return to society. It is hoped that by providing educational and job training, they will be ready to be placed into jobs or schools at the point of release, instead of running up against dead ends and turning ultimately back to the pattern of criminal behavior.

The VERA Institute has also begun a court-employment project, under which those convicted of offenses, with the approval of the court and the District Attorney's office, are provided with closely supervised training and employment. This program, which both protects society from people not ready to return to unsupervised life and offers hope to convicts, means more than a chance for a new life; it is an important step in cutting down on repeat offenders. Far from "buying off criminals," as was charged during the 1969 mayoral campaign, the use of outside help to work with offenders is one critical method of protecting our city from the danger of criminals.

There is, finally, one more vital step we have taken, and that is an all-out effort at public education. Unbelievable as it may seem, the same citizens who are so fearful of crime are often the greatest allies of the criminal—by failing to take elementary steps to protect their property. Half of all stolen cars in this country are taken because the keys were left in them—and in New York we estimate that as many as 25 per cent of all offenses against property are "crimes of opportunity," which take place only because people fail to protect their homes by locking their doors and avoiding tipoffs to burglars.

We have therefore started a citywide campaign to alert the citizenry to steps they can take. Ironically called the "Support Your Local Burglar" drive, it tells New Yorkers how they help criminals by failing to protect themselves. Linked with this effort is an experimental program to protect merchants by offering free advice from specially trained detectives who tell them of specific protections they can build into their establishments.

None of these steps, by themselves, will erase crime from city streets. The roots are far too deep for that. Poverty, injustice, lack of any visible opportunity, the forces in men's lives that turn them to crime—all this will be with us for a long time. But what we have discovered is that the practices and inertia of the past have crippled our efforts at law enforcement, and that only a total commitment on the part of the city, combined with an integrated approach to law enforcement, can begin to equip our police and our courts and ourselves to provide a safer city.

Whatever strategies are mounted to combat crime, the cost will be high. No amount of rhetoric, no words or phrases, no slogans, no denunciations, no messages to the people, to the Congress, or to state legislatures are going to make the slightest dent in crime rates unless they are backed by a real commitment of money. The first-year cost alone of the 4,000 new police added to the city quota in 1968–69 was $60 million. The current operating budget for the Police Department of New York City is $460 million. It will be well over half a billion dollars next year. And these are just the regular police costs; they do not include transit police, housing police, prison police, probation and parole, criminal courts, youth houses, Phoenix Houses for narcotics addicts, and all of the other correction and rehabilitation programs and facilities. And those costs, too, keep rising, as do the demands.

And yet, thus far we have not even begun to hear the kind of talk that is needed from federal and state leaders in terms of hard dollars if our hard-pressed cities are to be aided in their lonely battles against crime. The National Commission on the Causes and Prevention of Violence has painted us a chilling picture of what will happen without this support: cities will become armed camps, with their citizens living and working in fear. To prevent this fate—to gain the support we need—is a fight that all of the cities will have to make if the battle against crime is to succeed.

IX

The City and the State

IN NEW YORK, the Mayor and the Governor have a special tradition of commemorating the major religious holidays in the Judaeo-Christian tradition. Each December, sometime around Christmas and Chanukah, the Mayor writes the Governor a letter outlining the fiscal needs of the city for the coming year and describing the severe consequences that will result if the city does not receive a fair share of the taxes collected from the city and state. The Governor then acknowledges the needs of the city and describes the financial pressures on the state that will make such help unlikely.

In April, at about the time of Easter and Passover celebrations, the Mayor makes a pilgrimage to Albany, the state capital, to present the case for additional city money. The legislature leaders greet this request with a level of enthusiasm traditionally reserved for the bearer of such tidings. Then, at the last minute, the ritual ends with a sudden burst of intensive negotiations, and stop-gap measures are applied to carry over the crisis to the next year. Looking back at this custom, I think I understand why it is that, when I prepare for the Albany journey, I think of

Henry Hudson, who began his own journey as captain of the stately *Half Moon* and ended it in a rowboat somewhere off the coast of Canada.

This is a fair outline of the pageantry that surrounds the annual budget crisis in New York City. But the perennial struggle for adequate funds is no laughing matter. For we are not speaking of postponements of showcase projects or attractions. We are talking about cutting back admissions to the tuition-free City University system; shorter hours for museums and libraries; larger classes in our public schools; an end to the free-lunch program for the poorest students, often the only hot meal they get all day; restrictions on medical care for the needy and elderly; reductions in recreational programs in the summer for children who must stay in the city; and a general lowering of basic municipal services.

Nor is the New York City situation an isolated instance. In city after city, financial emergencies have become the rule, not the exception. Youngstown, Ohio, shut its schools in December 1968 when the voters rejected an education-bond proposal and the school system simply ran out of money; similar action was threatened in Detroit. In 1969 Newark, New Jersey, came close to completely shutting down its museum and library—two of the great cultural institutions in the state. Philadelphia found itself borrowing money to pay for police supplies, and a paper there carried the headline: "Philadelphia Fears City Is Going Broke."

The nation's cities, then, are in a serious fiscal crisis—and this crisis is not going to end soon. With rising demands for better public services, with constantly rising costs of goods and services for municipal programs, and with most cities at the effective limit of their power to raise revenues, cities are simply unable to supply these services through their own devices. In fact, according to one estimate, the cities of America will require, between 1967 and 1977, more than $260 billion in addition to what they can raise on their own. And unless this society wants to give up on its cities, that gap must be closed. The question is how? Where can the money come from?

In my view, much of this money can and should come from the federal government: directly, through a reordering of priorities and tax sharing, and indirectly, through financial incentives that encourage the participation of private enterprise in the social needs of the cities. But it is also clear that much of this assistance must come from the state. First, the state is the governmental unit closest to the cities, with direct access to the power to affect the basic condition of its citizenry. Second, the state and the city have traditionally shared most of the principal responsibilities: police, fire, sanitation, health, education, welfare. Finally, the state has severely controlled the ability of local governments to gather resources—through such devices as the ceiling on the debt limit and the real estate tax as well as numerous managerial controls, and the absence of home rule, which would enable the city to manage its own resources. With such drastic limits on city power, only the state can provide financial policies to ease the devastating impact of those controls. In most states lack of support has been the rule, but it can remain the rule no longer. The times simply do not permit it.

The pressures that have driven the city to its present state of fiscal dependence have been exhaustively discussed by a host of urbanists. Several waves of migration from the South, cresting under the pressures of World Wars I and II and the steady decline of agricultural jobs for the unskilled, filled the cities with millions of untrained and unskilled workers, black and white. The Depression pushed cities and states, for the first time, into the position of taking on the great responsibility of income maintenance for large numbers of people—a responsibility unprecedented in our national history. The rapid development of land within city boundaries drove the cost of housing sharply upward just at the time when the city, state, and ultimately federal governments recognized a responsibility to provide decent housing for all residents of the city.

Beyond these overpowering pressures, however, is something unique to large cities, which can perhaps be most sharply understood in the context of New York City. It is something I choose to call, with all deference to the economists, the *dis*economies of scale—in other words, the cost of being so huge, so densely populated, so concentrated.

Density does not deprive a city of a certain vibrancy, as on a day in early spring when New Yorkers come out of hibernation and flock to the parks and streets. There are authentic joys in city life. But nevertheless, density is responsible for inevitably higher costs for almost every conceivable service. Transportation is more expensive because it is so enormously complex to move people into the core city. Every morning, for example, 3½ million people are packed into the dozen or so square miles in midtown and downtown Manhattan. Buses and subways, built for a city with about 3 million fewer people, are always overcrowded at the rush hour; commuter roads, built before the last great suburban exodus, are a cause of near-insurrectionary dissatisfaction. And, as far as driving an automobile goes, the remark of our late Traffic Commissioner, Henry Barnes, is all too accurate: "The only way to get to the West Side," he said, "is to be born there." Average traffic flow is barely six miles an hour.

Yet where and how do you build? To dig up a city block creates massive chaos in the core city because of the maze of undergound cables, pipes, and wires that run beneath the streets. And this is why the cost factor of any improvement must reflect the sheer density of the central city.

Housing is a similar case. The land values on Manhattan are the highest in the world; in some areas land is so expensive that space is rented at $15 per square *foot.* Further, it is virtually completely occupied, either by housing or commercial interests. Every attempt at acquisition, for whatever purpose, brings severe resistance from those to be displaced, and for understandable reasons. There is no place else they can go, at a price they can afford, for the value of property is so enormously high.

Nor is cost the only factor. It is impossible to estimate how much dirtier our streets are because of illegally parked cars—we tow away 2,000 of them a week from midtown Manhattan alone—which prevent sanitation trucks from sweeping our streets and slow down the whole vital process of garbage collection. Yet illegal parking is, fundamentally, a reflection of density; legal parking spaces are difficult to find and the cost of parking in garages or lots is too high for many motorists. Thus, once again the sheer numbers of people in the city produce conditions that further increase our cost.

Finally, the enormous number of civil servants employed by New York produces constant pressure on our budgets. These men and women—350,000 of them—teach in our schools, clean the streets, fight fires, preserve order, work in public hospitals and colleges, clean the parks, drive our buses, repair water mains. For many years their salaries were far below a fair level, and it has always seemed to me blatantly unfair to keep costs down by exacting a compulsory subsidy from civil servants. Nonetheless, the very size of our public-employee force means that any pay raise will cost us dearly when multiplied through the whole system. Just for the 1970 fiscal year, for example, increased wages and fringe benefits for public employees will cost New York City $400 million, more than the total budget of many American cities.

Thus, size—added to all of the special problems of the big city—causes the city to continually exceed its revenue capacities. In some ways, the best analysis of the fiscal condition of the cities was made by the Red Queen in *Alice in Wonderland* when she said, "It takes all the running you can do, just to stay in the same place. If you want to get somewhere else, you must run at least twice as fast." Our dilemma is even worse. With all the running we do, our expenses still exceed our income. Here in New York City we have in the last three years put through revolutionary fiscal reforms. We have stopped borrowing on our future, we have brought a measure of order into our tax system, we have instituted a city income tax to broaden the revenue base, we have made the local tax structure more progressive, and we have even won approval for a tax on commuters. Yet with all this, in 1969 the city was $500 million short of adequate revenues—and there is virtually no city in America that has not and does not find itself in a similar condition. We look, then, to the state, and ask to what extent it is implicated in the perilous financial conditions of the city.

What we find in New York City, and what can be found in many other cities, is a pattern of three parts: first, total state control over the fiscal powers of the city; second, state-mandated programs that compel the spending of large sums of money by the city; third, a history of state underfinancing of the city in relation to both need and revenues received from the city, which has cost us literally billions of dollars.

By total control I mean that the city can neither increase taxes nor borrow money without the consent of the state legislature and, in some cases, by constitutional amendment. Not only does the whole pattern of taxation and state aid to localities depend on the decision of the legislature, but even municipal attempts to raise revenues to save itself must meet objections from legislators across the state. Thus, in 1966, when a commuter tax was proposed on those who live outside the suburbs but who work in the city, we had to win the support of legislators who represented precisely those districts whose citizens would be taxed for the first time. Under such circumstances, it was a genuine victory to have won what we did (a tax on commuters at less than half the rate at which city residents were taxed). But there are also important losses. At the start of 1970 the bus and subway fares were increased 50 per cent at a time when a third of the New York City work force was earning less than $100 a week. The fare was raised by a *state* agency after the Governor and *state* legislative leaders refused to permit the *city* to impose taxes to permit a twenty- or twenty-five-cent fare. By ourselves, we only had power to impose tolls and fees that would have fallen far short of the money needed.

Beyond absolute fiscal control over the city, the state frequently establishes programs that require substantial expenditures by the city. The most expensive examples are welfare and Medicaid (a program of medical care for the "medically indigent" of the state). Under this program, the state establishes the levels of financial aid and the city must then pay for the mandated share of the program. Significantly, most of these kinds of programs hit with particular impact in the big city. Most poor people are within the boundaries of the city; by definition, so are most of those "medically indigent," i.e., people who work at marginal jobs but for whom any serious illness would represent financial disaster. To force a contribution from the city, then, is equivalent to determining a massive share of the city budget without offering any alternative. For example, the Medicaid program requires the city to pay 30 per cent of the costs—a sum that will cost the city tens of millions of dollars. (This staggering amount does not even include the consequences of sharp changes in state and federal aid that brought large numbers into the system three years ago and then excluded many because of cutbacks in state and federal help. Inevitably, much of this burden will fall on the city hospitals.) The welfare program, a response to a national economic dislocation, costs the city more than $300 million of its own funds to supplement the income of the blind, the sick, and the dependent and disabled. New York State mandates a greater share of welfare costs on localities than all except one other state.

Then there is a collection of lesser mandated costs that are not so burdensome, but in their own way are even more irritating because they are slipped through the legislature in the closing hours when no one is looking. Example: New York City is forced to pay the maintenance costs of stations owned by the Long Island Railroad and located within the city. (This particular commuter railroad is now owned and operated by the state.) Another example: New York City must pay a portion of the salaries of state court judges. (New York City already totally funds its own three separate court systems.) And another: the city must pay for pension increases granted by the legislature over and above gains already won by careful collective bargaining and painfully included in an already exploding municipal budget.

The irony of this kind of policy—mandating programs that the state desires but for which the city must pay substantial portions—is that it flies directly in the face of virtually every study made on such programs. Three presidential commissions, including the recent task force of President Nixon's, have recognized that the cities of America simply cannot bear the continued costs of income dependency—that outside help, preferably in the form of a federal assumption of the full costs of public assistance, is required to relieve from the cities the disproportionate burden of welfare, whose sources are fundamentally national in nature. Yet in New York the local expense budget each year is burdened by such expenditures. Some forty states now at least recognize the unfairness of this local burden and, pending a federal takeover, have assumed the local cost. New York State should do the same.

But the cost to the cities of such requirements pale beside the most critical fact of city-state fiscal relationships: the persistent imbalance between the city's contribution to the state's tax revenues and state aid to the city.

The reasons for this condition are complex. First, they stem in part from the fact that at the time of the last important reforms in taxation and aid, the cities, because of rapidly rising real estate values and property assessments, were fully adequate to meet the needs of the citizenry. Fifty, even forty, years ago, as one study noted, "the city's fiscal tools were as adequate as those available to the state and federal governments." Moreover, the city was the center of virtually all critical economic activity, and its reach therefore encompassed those institutions that could best support city needs. In the intervening years, however, the same conditions that put large numbers of poor people into the cities drove businesses and individuals with economic resources out, and thus the pattern of city-state taxation and assistance, once all but irrelevant to the city, became a practical obstacle to an adequate measure of support.

Second, the state as the principal regulator of the resources of the city was naturally inclined to view the city, the center of economic activity, as a source of funds, rather than as a recipient. Economic conditions in rural and other areas of the state were severe even before the Depression, and there was a compelling need, particularly when the state entered the task of supporting public education and welfare, for a ready, massive source of funds. That, of course, was New York City. As we have already noted, the city currently sends $3 billion annually to Albany and receives only half that amount back.

Third, and often overlooked, is the fact that the state legislature, along with virtually every other legislature in the country, was malapportioned. Despite the population of the city, which until the migration to the suburbs was about half of the state's, rural representation was dominant. Not until the one-man-one-vote decisions did the city achieve anything approaching equitable representation in the state legislature. And that body had long since enacted a series of formulas for local assistance that was frankly and openly discriminatory—perhaps out of a conviction that the cities were somehow less deserving, perhaps out of a natural concern for the districts that the majority of legislators represented.

Whatever the cause, the result was a massive underfunding of the city at the very time when the fiscal resources of the city became strained. The large numbers of the unskilled now in the central cities were unable to find employment; those who had the skills to adjust to increasingly white-collar jobs did not live there. Thus, in the words of one commentator, "the city's economy [became] good at creating jobs for the kind of people who tend to live in the suburbs."

It is impossible to estimate with any accuracy how many billions of dollars in resources were lost to New York and to other large cities because of this gap in resources. We do know that from the time of the postwar period until recent reforms in New York's assistance pattern, the city contributed billions more than it received—and even counting state functions, the return to the city of tax dollars generated by it and collected in it by the state was shockingly inadequate. We know that in general the cities of America are in the same predicament as my own: between 1950 and 1966 revenues increased about 30 per cent while expenditures went up 44 per cent—and, inevitably, the debt of cities increased in that same period almost 59 per cent.

Even today, after significant improvements in the formula by which state aid is dispensed, serious discrepancies still exist. Aid to education, one of the most important kinds of state assistance, is still geared to real estate values in localities—a condition under which New York, with its enormous real estate values in Manhattan, is presumed more capable of financing its own educational system than other parts of the state, despite the more than a million students in its schools, despite the massive costs of educating students with language difficulties (there are over 125,000 pupils in the city schools whose primary language is not English), and despite the welter of educational problems that every study has shown to exist in a school system where hundreds of thousands of children come from poverty backgrounds, with neither a decent home life nor adequate educational background. Despite all this, New York still gets almost one-third less per pupil in state aid than the rest of the state—and federal studies have shown that other state legislatures treat their big-city school systems the same way.

This educational discrimination is carried through to the university level. New York City is the only city in the nation that supports a free university system, a system which has educated some of the most important citizens of our city, providing the bridge from poverty to opportunity. Its budget of $221 million requires outside help, particularly given the drive toward increased education on the part of black, Puerto Rican, and lower-income white students. Yet the state funding program provides less than a third of the level of help to the City University system that it offers to the State University—despite the vastly greater resources available to the state for educational purposes.

Finally, there is the inescapable fact that the city is a critical source of continuing support for the state, including people who do not live here and who do not even work here. It is obvious that the mass-transit system is of crucial importance to the millions who commute daily to the city; that pollution control is a health matter not just for the city, but for everyone, commuters and others, whose well-being is affected by continued air pollution; and that if the city declines economically and spiritually the well-being of the state is to that extent crippled. The cities continue to be viewed as burdens and problems—but it should never be forgotten that they are resources of untold value to the states. Investment in the health of the city, then, is the most important kind of investment the states can make, and it is a tragedy that this investment still seems to be ignored by the state when the time comes to substitute acts for rhetoric.

What, then, can be done to cure this imbalance?

First, states must grant home rule and permit the cities far greater flexibility in generating their own resources. There is in New York City a good example of Albany's prejudice blocking badly needed increases in money for the city. For at least a decade New York City has been asking the state for permission to establish off-track betting, whereby people could take part in state-authorized and controlled racetrack wagering at locations throughout the city. And for more than a decade the legislature has refused to act.

As far as anyone can determine, this opposition stems from the fact that it is somehow "immoral" to engage in gambling away from the track, although it is patriotic and civic-minded to gamble at the track, and the state also viewed it as "moral" to establish a lottery two years ago. In fairness, a more practical objection is rooted in the fear of losing admission fees to the track. It is also argued that poor people would wager a larger share of their income if off-track betting was legalized. To me, this objection seems specious. If the concern is with the financial affairs of lower-income people, then off-track betting should be encouraged, since it will save these people the cost of admission and transportation. Moreover, not having off-track betting does not stop gambling on the horses away from the racetrack; it only drives it into illegal operations, thereby assisting organized crime, and deprives the city and state of a proper share of the revenues.

Most important, at least to the city, is that legalization of off-track betting could bring New York an additional $100 million to $200 million every year—a vital increase in city funds that would be accomplished without resorting to increased taxation.

Given New Yorkers' overwhelming approval of this proposal, and given the certainty of important increased resources, there is simply no reason for Albany's continued opposition.

Such reforms, however, do not meet the basic need for increased money. They can help, but they cannot by themselves close the gap. To do this, we need nothing less than a major reform in fiscal structure, which has not been attempted by the state for a generation and which has left the city without adequate resources. I believe that this reform is a real possibility, both in New York and across the nation.

Briefly, it would require a revenue-sharing principle similar to that in which the federal government would set aside a portion of its revenues for a return to the state, without conditions or restrictions, to enable them to increase the level of their services. This proposal, which has been put forth by Walter Heller and endorsed repeatedly by the governors' conferences of both major political parties, is a sound one, and I endorse it. But there is no reason why such a proposal would not have equal validity if applied to the state-city relationship. The same basic principles apply—states have far more flexibility in raising revenue, they have a wider tax base, and they—not the cities—can set the rate and the source of taxation.

My proposal, which I have called Urbanaid and which for the third year I have pressed in Albany without success, would have the state set aside a measure of its revenues for return directly to localities, large and small alike. The amount returned would be flexible, depending on the population of the locality, its degree of self-taxation, and the peculiar needs of regions. Such a system would be easy to administer; it would not cut back on basic state services; and, most important, it would afford continuing and secure state support to the cities so that they could plan their budgets intelligently, without the prospect of perennial crises and recriminations. It would, of course, take much of the drama out of spring, since the Mayor would no longer be traveling to Albany for last-minute appeals for aid, but this loss would be tolerated, I think, by citizens who knew the basic level of municipal services would no longer be dependent on the decisions of a legislature that has shown its willingness to let localities bear the consequences of inadequate funding. This concept of local revenue sharing is, I believe, the single most important reform that could take place to redress the imbalance between the states and the cities of this nation. Combined with an intelligent program of federal revenue sharing, it would by itself reorder priorities in a critical fashion, reversing the slow, steady decay of local services and providing the tools to make the cities more livable.

In addition, the state can and must increase the political autonomy of the city. Both the New York City Council and the Board of Estimate are legislative, policy-making, fund-appropriating bodies. This twin legislative machinery provides a reasonable check on executive powers wielded by the Mayor, and yet almost every matter of importance—from the condition of the hospital system to the disposal of city pension funds to the hours our police work—must be decided by the state legislature. (Sometimes the same bill must be passed both in Albany by the legislature and in New York by the City Council before it takes effect.) This power even extends to the most specific managerial business, such as the right of sanitationmen to tag illegally parked cars that interfere with cleaning the streets.

These are operations which are completely funded and administered by the city and for which the state bears no burden whatever. And yet we are subject to the will of people who neither live in the city nor, often, know anything about its problems.

In the last mayoral campaign, authors Norman Mailer and Jimmy Breslin ran for citywide offices on a platform of statehood for New York City, and their views received a respectful hearing. This reflected New Yorkers' growing frustration and their feeling of impotence at having so little control over their own affairs, caused in good measure by Albany's rigid control of our political life. This frustration is compounded when we realize that we in the city are the chief financial supporters of state as well as of city services. The battle for home rule—the right to run our affairs—is going to grow in the coming years, and the state must begin to respond to it.

These are not the only reforms the states can make. They can, for example, redesign their aid to make it more relevant to the cities. While the state provides large sums of money for transportation, almost all of it is for highways. We need highways to increase economic opportunity in rural areas, but to offer massive highway funds is to the cities like offering sugar to a diabetic. There are already too many highways, which have damaged our cities far too much in the last three decades. What is needed is the kind of flexibility that permits cities to use transportation funds for *mass* transit—the urgent priority is moving large numbers of people through the city. (We have made a start in New York through the creation of the Metropolitan Transit Authority, which will at long last coordinate transportation policy to link up commuter lines, subways and buses, and highways in a coherent fashion. But we still lack the money to build subways and other systems fast enough and, even worse, to operate them at cheap fares once they are built.)

There are some who have said that these suggestions are visionary, that they depend on a change of attitude that will never take place in our legislatures. I do not believe this. First, these are eminently realistic, practical proposals rooted in the fact that, whatever we promise or intend, it will take financial tools to better our cities—tools that the state can help make available to our urban centers.

More important, I do not believe the states wish to continue to cede their legitimate, historical role as innovators to the federal government. Throughout modern history the states have been the crucibles of experimentation. Child-labor laws, workmen's compensation, and unemployment insurance were all at first the programs of far-seeing state legislatures, of which New York's was one, that were determined to meet the needs of the citizenry.

More recently that drive and spirit has been lodged in the federal government and, increasingly, in the cities. But I believe the states do have the capacity to act and that, despite all the years of inaction, they can make important decisions to improve the health of our cities. They have the resources and the capacity. What they lack is the will. With reapportionment giving the urban centers in New York State and elsewhere the representation they deserve, we can hope that there will be a new responsiveness to the conditions of the cities. For the cities have been speaking now, and their condition no longer permits inertia or indifference. Our states must make this commitment—for their sake and for the sake of their citizenry. Because without that commitment the sources of their strength, and ultimately the vigor of their people, will be inadequate. With that commitment the states can help both to salvage our cities and restore to themselves the appropriate role of progressive, vital institutions.

X

The City and the Federal Government

THE LAST FIVE YEARS have erased any doubt that the condition of our cities is an urgent national concern. Each of these five years has brought a new explosion of violence, new bloodshed and destruction, and new stunned realizations that the fabric of social order in our cities is straining dangerously. If for no other reason than the danger of explosive violence, Americans have become inescapably aware of the cities as an issue.

There are, however, other reasons, more fundamental and more persistent than violence. Riots are a spasmodic symptom: generational poverty, physical decay, and the loss of faith by the citizens of our cities are far more lasting, and far more dangerous, not only to them, but to the whole sense of national purpose and confidence that is at the core of a vibrant society. Perhaps most basically, the cities of America are increasingly becoming the typical national environment. The same metropolitan areas that held less than half of our citizenry at the turn of the century now hold three-fourths of them, and by the two-hundredth anniversary of the Republic that figure will be

80 per cent. To say, then, that the problems of the cities are not the responsibility of the federal government is to say that the life of most Americans is not the federal government's concern.

Finally, the federal government has already developed programs to meet some of the social problems of our cities, a commitment made well before the spate of Great Society legislation and well before the string of violent uprisings in the ghettos. The Full Employment Act of 1946 committed itself to the proposition that widespread unemployment could be overcome by necessary federal efforts. In our cities today there are at least 500,000 people who are totally without work and without the minimal skills to gain that work—the so-called "hard-core unemployed"—and if we count those who are employed full time at poverty wages or part time at sub-subsistence pay, the figure is far higher. Similarly, the National Housing Act of 1949—a bill passed fifteen years after the first national expression of responsibility for adequate shelter—declared as a federal goal the creation of "a decent home in a suitable environment for every American family."

Yet by any objective criteria this goal remains unrealized. As of 1966 more than 6 million housing units were "substandard" nationwide—i.e., either dilapidated, deteriorating, or lacking full plumbing. This figure, shocking as it is, does not even begin to define the full nature of the problem. Federal housing policy has led directly to the destruction of far more units than were built, with a consequent tightening of low-rent housing and increased occupancy of substandard housing by low-income families. (It has also been responsible for the destruction of sound neighborhoods, at a social cost of dislocation that we cannot measure.) This is not a strictly racial problem, for although 25 per cent of all Negroes in cities live in substandard housing compared to 8 per cent of all whites, there are, in numbers, far more whites in bad housing than there are Negroes—two and a half times as many in our core cities.

Thus there are explicit pledges of federal action that have not been redeemed. But this is not all. There is also the inescapable fact that the dilemmas afflicting our cities will not go away. To those who believe that a solution lies in flight to the suburbs, a presidential Report on the Suburbs, completed at the end of 1968, was a discouraging word, indeed. It found "a quiet crisis" in suburbia, a crisis composed fundamentally of wholly inadequate services, intolerable misuse of land, and an increasing number of badly planned, uncoordinated developments that contain the seeds of future decay.

This crisis, I think it is clear, was spurred in large measure by the accelerated flight from inner city to suburb, particularly in the years since 1945. In that time, to give one example, it is estimated that New York City lost 800,000 middle-income families who were seeking that "decent home in a suitable environment" that the inner city could not give them. In that same time, about the same number of families, largely poor and unskilled, came to the city in a wave of migration that has only recently leveled off. The consequences to the city are clear, but so are the consequences to the suburbs; at least, if they were not clear at the time of the urban exodus, they are clear now. There is a population explosion in small towns that lack the resources and services to plan adequately for growth because of unhampered land use that permitted the construction of enormous numbers of poorly planned and built developments, which, in the words of a folk song, are "all made out of ticky-tacky and they all look just the same." These isolated, unrelated towns and villages (more than 1,400 separate governmental units surround New York City) have no intercommunity communication and no effective methods of planning either open space or social services, controlling air pollution, preserving recreational land, or developing a plan for future growth.

These problems are only going to worsen if more and more families, unable to find satisfaction in the city, flock to the suburbs. Thus to ignore the city is to decree that crisis after crisis will afflict not just the big cities but all the metropolitan regions of America in the coming generation.

Finally, consider the federal government's responsibility for what has happened to the city, quite independently of any commitment to social justice. What helped to spur the suburban exodus? It was in large part the Federal Housing Administration's all-out effort to encourage home ownership in the years following World War II, principally through low-interest mortgages. This program, which brought suburban living within the range of millions of families, was to a great extent responsible for suburban flight, and it was also responsible for the pattern of virtually total residential segregation in the suburbs, since until 1949 the FHA refused vitally necessary insurance to any unsegregated housing area (in fact, it was not until 1962 that the FHA began to enforce a nondiscrimination policy).

Another key element in city-urban patterns was the enormous growth of spending for highways—spending that has now exceeded $60 *billion.* This program, the National Defense Highways Act, which has been described earlier, provided federal funds for highways at 90 per cent; with no federal funds whatsoever to aid mass transit, it was inevitable that states would take this available funding into account when deciding how best to link the burgeoning suburbs with the inner city. The consequence is clear to anyone who has tried to make his way through city streets: massive congestion, as cars inch along routes never designed for so many automobiles; increased pollution, as auto fumes account for much of New York's sulfur dioxide content; a hampering of mass transit, as city buses compete with automobiles for the inadequate street space; a direct decrease in sanitation, as parked cars make it difficult to collect refuse and all but impossible to sweep the streets.

My point is not that the people who designed this system could foresee the distant though inevitable consequences of such planning, even though there were those who warned. Lewis Mumford, the Cassandra of the cities, wrote in 1958 just after the passage of the National Defense Highways Act: "The most charitable thing to assume about this action is that they hadn't the faintest notion of what they were doing. Within the next fifteen years they will doubtless find out, but by that time it will be too late." It took far less than fifteen years to find out, but otherwise his prediction was sadly accurate. My point, rather, is that the federal government is directly implicated in the crisis of the cities through these and a variety of other acts, including a welfare system that all but guaranteed migration of the poor and a system of national priorities that simply did not include the growing urban crisis. It cannot escape responsibility for what has happened to the cities, and if it continues its present programs and policies it is going to become a silent accessory to the ultimate decay of our society. Its responsibility is bipartisan and nonpartisan; it is a consequence of misdirected basic structure—of inadequate financial aid, of blind assumptions, and of shocking indifference—that must change. The most that can be said at the moment is that federal officials do not question the premise that the need for help is critical.

Unfortunately, good intentions are not enough. What is needed is massively increased funding to the cities, a commitment to alter some deeply rooted habits of the federal bureaucracy, and a willingness to take some fundamental risks in coming to grips with the American city. It is a hard responsibility, particularly for an administration that is daily plagued with such legacies as the War in Vietnam and a foreign policy that guarantees it will be entangled in the affairs of dozens of nations. But it is the most critical domestic responsibility that confronts the national administration.

The nature of the change in the federal response to the cities must, I think, take three basic forms:

1. A reordering of priorities, reflected not in rhetoric but in the cold, hard spending of federal funds, channeling far greater resources back to the cities—through both

direct grants and the kinds of incentives used to promote developments in other fields regarded as critical by the federal government.

2. A reformation of the nature of federal programs, placing far greater autonomy within the province of the cities, and most particularly within the control of neighborhood and community groups, subject to reasonable and effective standards of performance.

3. A commitment not simply to participation in programs, but to the establishment of programs that use federal funds to create self-generating resources so that organizations can ultimately become reliant on their own ability.

I think each of these reforms is critical enough to merit a separate discussion.

Reordering Priorities: The people responsible for governing our cities have been aware for a long time—a lot longer than I've been Mayor of New York—that we were being choked by a lack of funds and that this lack of money was as serious as a lack of oxygen to a human organism. Without oxygen cells die, because they cannot replenish themselves, and they decay—and ultimately so does the life of a man. Without money communities die, because they are unable to rebuild themselves, to get the services needed to deal with health and housing, education and sanitation and elementary public safety. And if communities die or become stultified, so, ultimately, does the city.

That states the problem. The question is, where is the money coming from? My own answer, not original or particularly complex, is that it must come, in far greater measure than ever before, from the federal government. The federal government now is responsible for more than $190 billion a year in spending—more than one-fifth of the entire gross national product. It is, by an overwhelming measure, the gatherer and dispenser of the nation's public resources. It can, by a simple act of will, re-establish the order of importance of public programs, as it did following the launching of Sputnik in 1957, when the space program suddenly became second only to national defense as a recipient of federal funds.

Moreover, the federal government can, by its establishment of priorities, spark a massive shift of emphasis in the private sector. If it generates a demand for space research, that demand will fundamentally change the composition and thrust of every institution from electronics companies to graduate departments of universities—and thus, through a "multiplier" effect, the drive of the federal government almost inevitably becomes the drive of our most critical institutions, public and private.

The government, then, specifically the federal government, has the power to establish a national effort. The question is, what kind of priorities require alteration? The answer, in the first instance, lies in the major areas of federal spending.

Let us look first at defense spending. It is not only the most expensive federal effort, but it is also the most dramatic example of the way the federal government can shape the pattern of national effort by its own acts. By now, some of the results of twenty-five years of the cold war are becoming clear to us. Since World War II the United States has spent 1 trillion dollars—1 *trillion* dollars—on national defense, a figure that is all but incomprehensible. It is a thousand billion dollars, more than all the money spent by New York City and New York State since they were founded.

But it is a lot more than simply a staggering sum of money. It has many consequences.

First, it has stimulated prime use of the nation's scientific and technological elite by in effect suspending the operation of the market and guaranteeing the profits of companies engaged in defense (and, later, space) research. The sheer size of the military budget and the constant demands for new weaponry have produced what amounts to a fourth branch of government: the military-industrial complex, which has, since 1950, received more than $500 billion in defense contracts. I do not know how we can measure the extent of the influence of this "fourth branch," about which President Eisenhower warned in his farewell address in January 1961.

But I do know that it has meant an overwhelming imbalance in terms of where our scientific knowledge has been used, and the victims of that imbalance are the cities of the United States. Consider the condition of most city institutions: our schools are old, often with obsolete equipment and books (in 1960 some schools were using science texts that did not include any recognition that the atom had been split). Mass-transit systems, some of them built as long as sixty years ago, were overcrowded, filthy, and in general uncomfortable if not unbearable in the summer. (There is a story—perhaps apocryphal—that an American Indian, on riding a commuter railroad out of New York City, exclaimed, "My ancestors used to attack trains like this!") The cost of housing has soared so high that each year it costs 8 per cent more to build the same number of housing units.

There is not one of these areas that could not achieve substantial, perhaps revolutionary progress by the application of modern technological help. We already know that computerization can lower crime rates by dispatching patrol cars in accordance with a predictable pattern of crime. We know, too that computers can improve hospitals immediately by providing swift diagnosis and a minimal level of patient observation, thus freeing nurses and doctors from routine burdens. We believe—with good reason, given the accomplishment of technology elsewhere—that it could devise wholly new systems of mass transit, develop housing techniques to drive construction costs down, provide new kinds of teaching equipment that would enable us to break free of lockstep instruction in our schools, and solve the question of disposing the solid wastes that threaten to engulf the city in a sea of garbage.

But we have not had the chance to find out because, in large measure, the technology of modern America is exclusively at the service of defense and aerospace concerns—a consequence of federal policy that has made massive amounts of money available for these pursuits.

This policy goes beyond pure procurement of goods and information. In money spent on Research and Development, which more than anything else reveals to the nation's industries what the government wants developed, the imbalance is enormous. Of about $20 billion allocated to R&D this year, 90 per cent is being spent on military research and development for new weaponry. Yet each year we delay solving urban problems is another year of decay—for our schools, hospitals, neighborhoods—and another year of hardship for the cities.

This imbalance is not, however, the only consequence of our defense policies. Somehow, the mere expenditure of such large funds tends to perpetuate itself even as the meager amounts spent on our cities defines the limit of "proper" federal outlays. It is almost as though a law of political inertia governed national priorities: since we have always spent 50 or 60 per cent of our federal budget on defense, we should never spend less; since we never spent more than $1 billion for urban housing, we cannot think of doubling or tripling that sum. I have seen this at work in Congress, where I served for seven years. One day a $70 billion defense budget (it is now about $80 billion) would be passed without a murmur of dissent on the House floor, sometimes without even a quorum being present, and a day later there would be earnest and skeptical debate about a $10 million rat-control bill or about the premise that the federal government should engage in the "socialistic" business of assisting elementary and secondary education.

Similarly, the vast sums themselves seem to excuse flagrant misuse of money. I remember that each year in Washington, ex-Senator Paul Douglas used to display item after item bought by the military at ten to forty times the competitive cost without generating a trace of the concern expressed at the discovery that somewhere in a big city a family was cheating the welfare department out of $20 a week. Only recently a former Budget Bureau official disclosed that more than $15 billion in defense contracts had either been canceled, phased out, or found to be 75 per cent unreliable. Had one-one-thousandth of this sum been found to have been misspent for education or in the poverty program, the investigations would be lined up by the dozens. Somehow, however, the defense industry is immune from such scrutiny.

I have focused on the defense budget because it is the most dramatic—and certainly the most expensive—example of a governmental priority that becomes sacrosanct, free from the kind of public scrutiny that such outlays of money normally receive. I have also emphasized it because of its cost. New Yorkers pay $3 billion a year in taxes to support the War in Vietnam, and they pay $6 billion more for the military budget. That amount is 50 per cent more than our *total* city budget for police, for nurses, for schoolteachers, firemen, engineers, park employees, professors, sanitationmen—for all of this and every other part of our budget.

As I have already noted, both of my opponents in the 1969 campaign argued that the Vietnam War was not a relevant issue. I said it was, and I still do. I believe it is critically relevant to New York City—and every other part of the country—and have said so since March 1965, when I made my first public talk on the escalating error of our policy in Vietnam.

I asked then for an end to our country's military involvement and mentioned the channels of diplomacy then open as the means of orderly withdrawal. I questioned the nature of the government we were supporting and tried to point out that our unilateral military involvement was totally contrary to our professed policies of collective security since World War II.

That speech, given in Michigan, was not very popular at the time, but I thought then that the continued preoccupation with the War in Vietnam would inevitably produce division at home. If anything, I was far too optimistic. At the very time when pressures for progress at home have mounted, the war has steadily and continually drained not only our resources but our attention and our will. To hear now from high federal officials that even an end to the war will produce no progress—to hear that new ventures into military spending will continue to drain this money—is simply incredible. And it cannot be accepted as national policy.

But it is just as incredible that we should have spent more than $60 billion for highways while the inner-city and commuter mass-transit systems are at the point of extinction. It is even more upsetting to realize that in the years since this discrepancy has become clear we still have not moved to alter the most flagrant imbalances in our transit expenses.

For example, in the current budget, the federal government plans to spend $5.1 billion on ground transportation. Of this amount, $4.9 billion—or more than 95 per cent—is on highways. The primary reason is that this money is part of a highway trust fund whose money has been accumulating for a dozen years and which is devoted exclusively to highways. The same law of political inertia that puts our defense establishment beyond review also decrees that this trust fund remain inviolate. In fact, when a group of senators and congressmen suggested that the state be permitted to spend this money on either highways or mass transit, as they saw fit, it was roundly rejected. In other words, the Congress *mandated* the continuation of policies that forced cities to choose between the further choking of city streets and pollution of the air or no transit help at all. This kind of priority, built into our federal legislation, is the kind of undramatic, mechanical, unexciting legislation that does more to harm the cities than all of the rhetoric about meeting the urban dilemmas does good. And it is precisely this approach that must be changed.

There is far more. For example, the natural—or should I say, as a city dweller, unnatural—preference of single-family residential units as opposed to multiple dwellings has led to a persistent imbalance between federal subsidies (in the form of FHA mortgages) for private suburban homes and similar subsidies for inner-city housing. Through a process of double-think that I have seen but still do not understand, federal money is readily available to "subsidize" mortgage payments for private homes but far less readily available for the building of city apartments for middle- and low-income families. Somehow it is socialistic or un-American to help a poor or working family move into an apartment, particularly if the unit cost of the apartment is more than $20,000. Yet the financing of $30,000 and $40,000 homes in suburban developments is in the best traditions of the Founding Fathers.

The logic is cloudy, but the results are clear. In the thirty-one years of subsidized housing for the cities, a total of only 800,000 units has been built. In roughly the same period, more than 10 million FHA-insured homes were built for suburban families. There are, of course, many problems connected with housing in the city: the need to find builders, the far more restricted land space, the time lag between proposal and building (sometimes more than ten years), and the fact that suburban development can plan on a clean slate. But it is still true that in simple priority terms, it is city housing that has been the stepchild of the federal government.

I think the basic point is now clear. Put simply, the federal government has never regarded the city *as such* as a matter of priority. It has been concerned with the people who live there—with their health and more recently their housing and education. But a city is more than just the people who live in it; it is an interrelated, organic center of life. For too long we have thought of the city as simply a place where a lot of people live. But you cannot help a city with that kind of thinking. You cannot build miles of highways through an urban center and think you have helped transportation if in fact you have simply displaced families, cut down a neighborhood, and increased pollution and congestion. You cannot build housing and think you have helped people if in fact your program tears down more than it builds, creates barracks through poor design and inadequate funding, and builds without concern for people. And you cannot help a city only by spending to treat effects and consequences; you must be willing to treat causes and conditions before they become crises.

Thus, the first urgent necessity is for a new federal policy—one that puts the city on a level of top priority—as important for the 1970's as defense was in the late 40's and space a decade later. It is for the federal government through new commitments to put the city in the center of national concern and to recognize that just as the farm, or labor, or military security demanded a mobilization of resources, so the city demands that kind of help today. It is not simply a matter of redressing the enormous gap between funds flowing out of cities and funds flowing into them—it is a matter of protecting and improving the quality of life for most American citizens in the coming years.

Reforming the Nature of Federal Programs: The structure of federal assistance in solving social problems is a direct outgrowth of the New Deal and Great Society concepts of assistance. To oversimplify it, this concept includes certain basic features: first, fairly stringent federal-agency control of how the money is spent—a tradition reflected in the "grant-in-aid" approach to federal assistance, which includes a limitation on how the funds are to be spent and the way in which a program must be structured and administered; second, a consequently obsessive concern with the details of such a program, a concern that on occasion overshadows worry about what the program is actually supposed to be doing; third, an attitude that holds that the way to solve difficulties with one program is to set up another one, with little real attempt to coordinate or to simplify the operation of the programs.

Let me give some examples. The federal urban-renewal program was aimed at clearing slums and building new housing—a program that grew out of the conviction that the way to improve the lives of poor people was to build new homes for them. The concept of asking the people living in the neighborhoods to be renewed how they felt about it was never really explored. It was simply assumed that those who had the power to plan and build knew what their "clients" wanted. Further, by placing a series of rigid cost formulas on the housing, it insured that not nearly enough units could be built to satisfy the needs of big cities. And yet because of the nature of top-down federal control there was almost no flexibility in the program, so that, to give one flagrant example, an entire site had to be cleared of existing housing before new homes could be built.

Now consider the consequences of such a program. Neighborhoods that had built up a pattern of stability and community—in which people lived and worked and shopped and knew each other—were often destroyed by decree. In fact, as it developed, the very possibility of turning neighborhoods into urban-renewal sites was enough to cause merchants and owners to consider selling to avoid a situation in which the government would order people to move and pay them sums vastly below what their properties were worth.

Then, since there were inevitably inadequate sums to build new housing, the residents of communities, particularly working-class and poverty-level people, found themselves out of their neighborhood with no place to go. The urban-renewal policy was very good for tearing buildings down, but it was far less successful in building new housing because of lack of money and the fact that delays between city and Washington meant higher construction costs and fewer units to be built with available money. Nor did it achieve an outstanding record in locating displaced tenants in new housing.

Finally, because of strict federal controls, the biases of those in power governed much of the program. Design was considered irrelevant; poor and middle-income people, the attitude was, should grateful for any housing built. Thus, in many units there were no doors on closets, no play areas for children except for sterile playgrounds, and, of course, no places for people to gather, such as

standing in the process that without adequate levels of funding it will make little difference which direction it moves.

This basic change, while important, is not difficult to make. It requires only mechanisms within our cities to use resources and plan development. The Model Cities committee is one such device. So are Community Development Corporations—units elected and run by residents of neighborhoods, financed by a small amount of federal seed money and by private contributions and loans, which would in effect plan, in the tradition of town-hall democracy, for the development of neighborhoods. This kind of corporation, proposed by such persons as the late Robert Kennedy and Charles Percy and supported by such diverse spokesmen as Senator John Tower and the Congress of Racial Equality, would have the virtue of being a central point for the coordination of the disparate federal programs that are now administered haphazardly and with insufficient citizen involvement.

A community corporation could put Head Start and day-care facilities together; it could combine community health facilities and job-training centers; it could serve as a central point to coordinate all the resources available through federal and private help with all the citizenry and their problems. It could also serve as the center for the neighborhood city hall, thus linking the efforts of individual neighborhoods with the agencies and departments of the city as a whole.

There is nothing utopian about this plan. In fact, even without community corporations, just such a program was started privately in Bedford-Stuyvesant under the aegis of Robert Kennedy. With a small amount of funds from the federal government, help from the city, a generous foundation grant, and the cooperation of some of the country's largest corporations, the Bedford-Stuyvesant Restoration Corporation has begun to tackle a whole range of problems in this subcity of 450,000 people. Its initial two years of performance have served as a demonstration that such efforts, without bureaucratic controls, can be effective. It is the kind of reform most necessary if federal assistance to the cities is not to be defeated by the sheer size and distance of the layers of government.

Finally, there is the concept of revenue sharing long endorsed by Walter Heller, former chairman of the Council of Economic Advisors, which has now achieved favor across the political spectrum. As one who has offered a similar proposal to the state government, I am in full agreement that this plan should be extended to the federal government. (I have, in fact, submitted a specific revenue-sharing proposal to Washington.) In brief, the idea is to set aside a share of federal funds collected through the personal income tax (1 or 2 per cent in the first years) and put them in trust for states and cities. Distribution would be on the basis of a series of considerations: population, degree of effort on the part of states and localities to tax themselves, and a guaranteed share to those states least able to help themselves.

Such a program would have a number of advantages, particularly if the revenue went, at least in part, directly to cities through bloc grants. First, it would help redress the kind of imbalance through which New York City finds itself without the use of its own resources to solve its problems.

Second, it would prove a powerful help in providing

steady, long-term funding to overcome the inevitable gap between the city's expenses and its revenues, thus ending the need for the inevitable annual confrontations and crises.

Third, it would give a powerful force to the cities in increasing the kind of municipal services that they alone provide—in schools, in hospitals, in sanitation, in crime fighting. In these areas, where at least a large portion of the problem is a simple lack of money, revenue sharing between Washington and the cities would make for an immediate improvement in the basic operation of city services. In addition, program grants could be earmarked by Washington for special innovative programs on an experimental scale to encourage the search for new solutions.

Self-Generating Resources: For most of my public life I have been a strong supporter of programs to improve domestic conditions. Along with others, I have supported the efforts of the poverty program to provide jobs, daycare facilities to children of working parents, and the extention of Head Start and Community Action projects. Yet this does not mean there is no room for improvement. And one of the most serious flaws in federal efforts, particularly in the poverty area, is the lack of emphasis on self-generating resources—i.e., the government's refusal to run the program by a grant of money that can be invested for future growth.

Consider what happens to a poverty grant for a demonstration program in a neighborhood: its funds are used to rent office space, purchase supplies, and provide salaries for the staff members necessary to carry out the program, be it a neighborhood health center, youth work, or

Head Start. At the end of the twelve- or eighteen-month grant, the program's funds run out; the participants must then go back to the funding agency and ask for a new grant.

The history of the poverty program reflects the problem. Inevitably, the vagaries of the federal budget or local politics can jeopardize such a grant, regardless of its success. The Child Development Group of Mississippi showed us one example of this. Because of the activist nature of the program, its challenge to traditional educational patterns, and its determination to battle segregationist patterns, Mississippi political forces launched an all-out drive against it—a drive that was ultimately successful in removing the program from the control of its original founders.

Even without political battles a lack of funds can and has cut short important gains made by such organizations. Time after time, in New York and in other cities across America, programs that had just begun to break through the inertia of communities were abruptly terminated or drastically reduced because funds had been cut or because federal officials felt it more important to begin other kinds of programs in other cities. The consequence of this kind of piecemeal funding is sharp and clear: increased dependence on federal and other funding agencies, inability to plan for long-range efforts, and, above all, an inability to establish a secure base for the development of neighborhoods.

One answer to this problem, and one that deserves serious consideration, is to begin moving toward the kind of programs that can develop self-generating resources so that local communities need not depend on governmental sources of wealth. For example, there is no reason why community corporations could not be permitted to invest federal seed money in neighborhood-run cooperative stores and industries in order to turn an investment into a permanent source of income for the community. There is no reason why they, or similar organizations, could not become the "landlord" of low- and middle-income housing, using the steady income from rent to build more housing or to provide other improvements for a neighborhood, from parks to hospitals.

The key, I think, is to recognize that it is far better to end dependence on government than to perpetuate it; far better to encourage individual and community independence than to continually tie improvements to a government which, however well intentioned, cannot respond as effectively as the citizens directly involved with the development of a neighborhood. It is ironic that in the decades of debate between "liberals" and "conservatives" so little attention was paid to the kind of fusion of concepts that provides an initial stimulus from the government, together with an effective mechanism to encourage economic, and ultimately full, independence from government bureaucracy. It seems to me that such a program, encouraged by the federal government through the investment of seed money in the community and by offering incentives to private industry to work with neighborhood groups, could be a vital source of growth for the cities at little cost to the taxpayers—and a convergence of these two worthy goals ought not to be neglected without a try.

XI

A Final Word

THE MESSAGE of Part II of this book is that our cities need help. They need money, desperately—money to pay schoolteachers, policemen, nurses, doctors, and the men who keep the streets and parks clean and the museums and libraries open. And they need far more than money. They need essential, root changes in their method of government to bring them in line with the twentieth century. They need government that is willing to risk political capital to give citizens a chance to control their own lives. They need the courage to say that basic methods of operation have not been working and must be scrapped.

But at the bottom line, they must have resources, because without them all reforms will be meaningless.

What good will it do to establish links between the city and its neighborhoods—if those links only serve to exchange demands from neighborhoods and confessions from the city that it is unable to act?

What good will it do to bring modern management methods into city government—if those methods disclose clearly that the city is facing inevitable bankruptcy each year unless resources are diverted?

What good will it do to design educational programs that break through environmental barriers—if the city cannot hire the teachers to put those programs to work?

It sounds, I know, as though this kind of approach is an attempt to explain away city failures. It is not. We have had setbacks in New York City, but we have had dramatic successes as well in basic city policy—in transportation and economic development, in crime fighting and environment control—even without some ultimately essential changes. And we can continue to innovate even if we continue to be left without resources.

But the fact is that such requests are not demands for handouts—they are demands that the resources generated by New York and every other city be retained instead of being used to subsidize every other priority of America.

If it is really important to spend $80 billion a year on the military-defense empire, then let Congress begin to tax the profits of the companies involved—not drain money out of the schools and neighborhoods of the city.

If it is really critical to pay farmers not to grow, then let them limit that subsidy—not cut job-training and housing programs.

If it is really vital to build a $60 billion highway system, then let it be paid for by those who use those roads—not by starving the mass-transit needs of the city, which grow more urgent every year.

For what has happened now is that the city has always been expendable. After the rheotric dies down, after the promises fade, we always find the cities of America cut out of the money. It is always summer job programs, housing programs, education-aid programs that are slashed in the name of economy—not the pork-barrel legislation establishing yet another military base in the hometown of a congressional committee chairman.

It is time that that kind of imbalance stopped.

It has to stop.

Because time has run out. Our cities will either be saved—now—or they will not be saved at all.

That is what this book is about. But more important, that is what this country is going to be about in the coming ten years or so. And it is up to all of us to see that our country makes the right choice.

Index

Index

Index

Index

Index